Anne Skare Nielsen   Henrik Good Hovgaard

AWAKEN YOUR FUTURE SENSE

Learn how to predict and design the future
for yourself, your business, and our civilization

May the force of the future be with you

UNIVERSAL
FUTURIST

Welcome to the most important game of our time

A pessimist says:
"It's always darkest just before blackout."

An optimist says:
"It's always darkest before dawn."

A tourists says:
"Well, well" and goes exploring no matter if it's light or dark.

A futurist says:
"It doesn't matter if it's light or dark. Let's get moving and create something great!"

This book will awaken your future
sense and invites you to play the most
important game you'll ever take part in:
the Game of the Future.

It teaches you to think and act like
a futurist – a curious, visionary,
constructive and motivating individual,
who uses knowledge, intuition and
practical experience to sense, predict
and design the future for the better.

After you've read the book, it's up to
you to do the next right thing. The
more radical a future you see, sense og
believe in, the more radical the change
– for you and the rules of the game.

And then you become
the game changer!

Introduction

Step into the universe of the future as if it were your very own analogue computer game. Listen to the future calling you.

Every level of the game teaches you how to predict and create the future out there in the real world. Just like a digital computer game, you move through different levels advancing in difficulty in your aim to become a true futurist and game changer.

You move on to the next level when you've learned what you need to know about yourself. The most important question is this: "Who are you in the world?" Who does the world need you to be? Expect drama and resistance. You are going to destabilize the status quo and challenge the old ways.

The gains are substantial! We want you to work out who you long to be and spice up your calling, your magic. We want you to identify the annoying framework that you must rebel against in order to make way for the energy you need to change the world for the better.

The distance between a person's ability to imagine and visualize something and his or her creative powers to make it happen has never been shorter. Your time is now! We are not human doings, we are human beings. Community and individuality are not opposites sides in a story, they are each other's prerequisites – they're part of the same story. So, when you get your shit together, there really are no limitations as to what you can accomplish, with others, just by being you.

'Me in the future' is and forever will be the best and most motivating topic. The only remaining question is whether or not you are ready to embark on this dramatic, exciting, dangerous and strenuous adventure?

Come a little closer…

Just a little closer…

A little closer still…

Now, you take the lead.

Welcome to the Game of the Future!

The Game of the Future

Chapter 1
The Game of the Future

Wake up your future sense and join this quest to change the rules of the game, so that everyone can win and no one loses.

People who study and research the future are called 'futurologists.' You are welcome to use the term yourself. Another term we use a lot is 'futurist,' which in Danish has a funny pun in the word 'fut,' meaning 'pep.' And so we really need FUTurists, because the coming years are going to be so damn epic! Everything you set out to do will be a success.

All the problems we're dealing with now will be resolved.

That dream you have of creating something big before you die will come true.

The worries that keep you up at night you won't even remember in the future.

And in the coming years, you will become more skilled, richer and freer and make new friends from all over the world.

The best thing? You will be able to help others become and achieve the same, while deep in your heart you feel a calm telling you that struggling to solve complex tasks and problems means fighting the right fight. It will feel like coming home – to yourself.

In the history of time, there's never been a shorter distance between a persons ability to visualize something and then creating something to materialize it and make it happen. The time it takes to overcome the hassle and annihilate the obstacles standing in-between your visionary ideas and creating something real becomes shorter and shorter.

The only requirement for obtaining a free and imaginative future is that you ditch the rule-abiding caretaker mindset and bring on your rebel game. So, grab your lightsaber, call Master Yoda and let's meet at the bar on Tatooine. Until then, practice the techniques that we give you and prepare to conquer your future vantage point.

The Game of the Future is open for everyone across age groups and educational backgrounds. It doesn't matter where you were born, where you live, what experiences you carry with you, if you are an old stager or are still green as grass in the ways of life. If you want to play the Game of the Future, you're more than welcome to join us.

The Game of the Future – So, What's the Idea?

The Game of the Future takes place in a world that is constantly moving. You can't observe it passively. You need to be an active gamer and fellow player who collects points and loot enough to improve the game. We will give you the necessary tools and help you train the skills you need to win the Game of the Future.

Seen from the outside, the game might seem complex. The future is out there somewhere, and so the game is never-ending as there will always be new players and new knowledge. One thing's for sure: It will be messier and more chaotic and you should expect the unexpected. For that reason, a lot of people opt out of the game early on, either because they confuse chaos with a lack of structure or because they assume that the reward will only come if they work really hard or when finally they get their shit together. This is the mindset of the rule-abiding caretaker and it will only make the future more heavy and confusing, for holy moly, do we have a lot of crap that needs fixing and a makeover.

In the future, it is absolutely essential to have fun. If you don't have fun, you lose – no matter how great your results.

If you settle and play by the rules, you will also lose. The rules of the past should be followed if they make sense. If they don't, you must change them. The rules you get to begin with were defined by the players in the past, but most of them only made sense in the game that they were playing back then.

You win the Game of the Future by having fun, changing or updating the rules for the better as you create something magic and awesome – together with others. So you should make sure to install the rebel mindset. It's actually very easy. Just say it out loud: "I choose to be a rebel!"

Come on, say it: "I choose to be a rebel!"

Thanks! Consider it done!

From now on, if you're ever in doubt, expect magic. All rebels do.

The game will automatically place you in situations that require you to solve relevant tasks and annoying challenges, which you can only accomplish by using and training your own insight. The game will keep throwing the same frustrations at you until you fully grasp the thing(s) you need to realize and release within yourself.

The Game of the Future: An Overview

The game of the future is constructed with seven levels and two modes to play.

When you have built a bridge between the Tribal and the Planetary modes, you win!

Future Magic
You have now become
A GAME CHANGER
And you know how to build a bridge between Tribal and Planetary
LEVEL 7
Visualization and creation: Be who you are, upgrade your skills and become richer and freer
LEVEL 6
Conquer your vantage point: Who does the world need you to be?
LEVEL 5
The seven demons: Don't swallow the bait, keep your energy levels high and stay focused
LEVEL 4
The game changer: You become the future you spot
LEVEL 3
Magic & irritation: Navigate the future and take a knock when you get lost
LEVEL 2
The Taboo Troll: Face your worst fears and step into the adventure
LEVEL 1
From MBA to MBS: Wake up your future sense and find your way on the planetary game board
TRIBAL
Success = Few winners, a lot of losers + we're playing by the rules of the past
PLANETARY
Success = Everyone wins, nobody loses + we're playing to improve the rules
MORE
BETTER
TUTORIAL
Play the game using the most important game changer of our time
Magic moments
The Piss Ant
The Dark Demon
Complex Rex
The Humping Troll
Stormtroopers
The Eraser
The Procrastinator

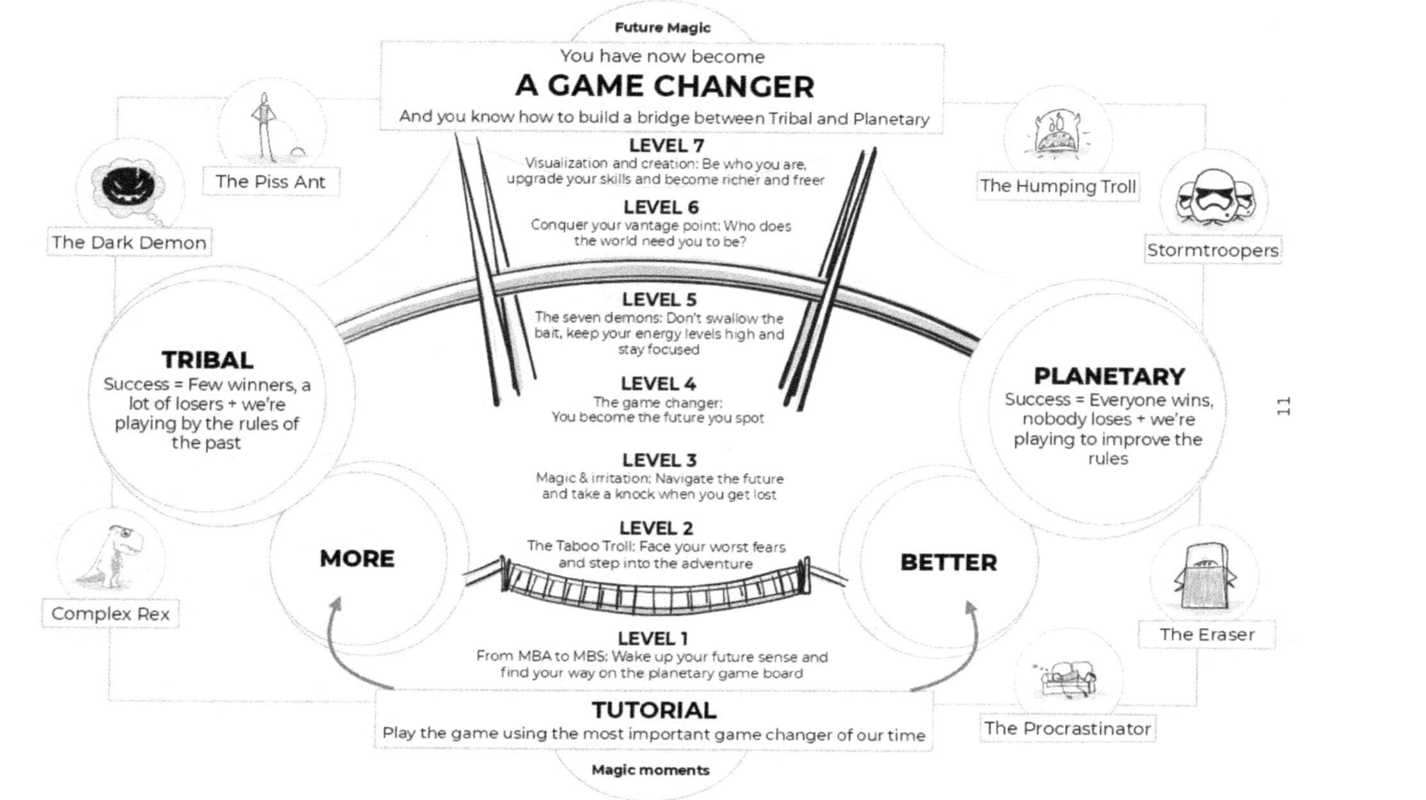

11

Basically, the Game of the Future is about to things: visualization and creation.

The game trains your ability to imagine and visualize the future, and in order to win, it dares you to dream big, create visions and execute. If at one point you can hear yourself thinking, "I don't see this" or "I can't imagine that," you are back to square one in the Game of the Future.

If you decide to hold on and maintain your course, however, you gain prospect and light. Enlightenment. In other words, a great story of an adventure in which you are the star.

In combining your visions and creative powers, you will become one of those people, who choose themselves, and you will enjoy what you see and know that you didn't just analyze and talk about the future – you actually took action and responded to it. You didn't settle for playing by the old rules, you broke the rules when it was necessary and you improved them for the better. You didn't just copy someone else's dream or knocked out the competition. You paved the way and allowed others to follow your footsteps. With your light you will be able to see where you've made a positive impact on your own life, on the world and on your friends.

And because the adventure is also an inward exploration, you've won the gift of enlightenment, of insight. You have taken your troubles, issues of irritation and frustrations and looked at them from another perspective. You learned what you needed to know and then let them go. You have faced and come to terms with your taboos, you have looked your inner demons in the eye and overcome your worst fear. Maybe you didn't accomplish everything you set out to do, but you sure did the best you could. You can look back on your life and into yourself and see very few regrets.

Mark our words: Your ego will love the Game of the Future, but you will never win, if you let your ego spinning the wheel. Greed and narcissism do not make a winning team in the future. If you are kind, humble, a little insecure, often in doubt and have very big dreams and you love to see others winning without pushing for a sidekick medal to yourself, rest assured that the Game of the Future loves you already. The future is all about community: love, friendship, empathy, the willingness to help. Sacrificing yourself without becoming a martyr or victim and making sure that we can all get safely across the bridge to the future.

How To Win the Game of the Future

Just like any other great game, you can advance in the Game of the Future as your skills improve. The game consists of a tutorial (for practicing) and seven levels.

Tutorial – Play the game using the most important game changer of our time.

Level 1 – From MBA to MBS: Wake up your future sense and find your way on the planetary game board.

Level 2 – The Taboo Troll: Face your worst fear and step into the adventure.

Level 3 – Magic and irritation: Navigate the future and take a knock when you get lost.

Level 4 – The game changer: You become the future you spot.

Level 5 – The seven demons: Don't swallow the bait, keep your energy levels high and stay focused

Level 6 – Conquer your vantage point: Who does the world need you to be?

Level 7 – Visualization and creation: Be yourself, upgrade your skills and be richer and freer

Tutorial

Before things get serious, you need to learn how to play the futurist.
In the tutorial section, you can rehearse playing the entire game using
our all-time favorite game changer "from 'more' to 'better.'" This is
the most simple way to create the future.

"From 'more' to 'better'" takes its point of departure in the game of
the past, the Tribal mode, where players are constantly hunting for
'more, more, more' and consequently are afraid of running out of
resources, money, etc. In the Game of the Future, you've got to make
something 'better' for more people using the right resources. Per
definition, you've already got the things you'll need. You just need to
realize and figure it out and then learn how to bring them into play.

Level 1

The game consists of two modes: Tribal and Planetary. The Tribal
mode is the old and very well-known zero-sum game. Planetary is the
new mode that you must find a way to change and make an impact
on. When we choose to play the Game of the Future, we become
the game changers, who build the bridge from "entitlement to
enlightenment." And we will leave all feelings of entitlement, offence
and vengeance behind and choose to see the future from a better
and more enlightened perspective. The enemy you're fighting in the
Game of the Future is not, surprisingly, 'the others.' It is yourself. Your
habits. Your practice. Your autopilot. If you play to beat everyone else
the shit out of the game, you loose! The first level, therefore, teaches
you how to get to know your own brain, since it's both your best friend
and your adversary.

You will also learn the reason why more often that not it's futile to
change your behavior in the now. Instead, the battle must be fought
in your visions for the future. By creating new stories, spotting trends,
visualizing magic moments, meeting your future with an open mind
and becoming the game changer you were born to be, you can re-

program your brain to lead you wherever you to need to be. So, make sure you dream big!

Level 2

On the bridge to the magical future stands a troll. It's the Taboo Troll, the evil cousin of the trend, whom you need to confront in order to pass. Confronting the Taboo Troll means facing your worst fears, including the biased opinions, your old habits and die-hard thoughts. The more established you are in your vantage point (the place from which you view the world), the more you've got to loose and the harder it will be to actually cross the bridge. But if you feed the beast to make it full, you will be set free. Without baggage and painful superstition, you are now free to move around in the Game of the Future and conquer a new and much better vantage point.

Level 3

On Level 3, you will learn that in the future there is no such thing as right or wrong decisions. There are, however, lots of endless dilemmas demanding to be explored and examined.

This is where you make decisions. You will 'meet' your decisions, because they are out there. And when you do, it's your job to make them the right decisions. Deal with your shit and take responsibility so you don't forward the unpleasant decisions to the-future-you. The-future-you has a lot on its plate already, so the present-day-you needs to choose what's best and right to do with the time and opportunity at hand. Accept the fact that you might fuck it up, and instead of stressing over right or wrong, you'll use magic moments and irritation to navigate with.

Know that magic will lead the way. And irritation will snap you back into your seat. The right decision is the one you make the right decision.

Level 4

In the tutorial, we lent you a trend as your game changer. On Level 4, you will find your own. And in order to do this, we will give you a quick brush up on how to spot trends. And then it's up to you to find and identify the trend that makes the future zoom in on you. Your game changer has to be both magical and irritating and provide opportunities to change the rules of the game. When you've found your game changer, you've come a really long way!

And when you act on it – meaning if you decide to do something about it and change the rules of the game – you become the game changer! The most epic player in the game!

Level 5

The Taboo Troll on Level 2 is the first challenge in the parade of monsters that you have to face in the game. On Level 5, the demons wake up. They will see how you try to shake the world, how you sprinkle your joy and energy and share your vision and creative powers with others. You are free and work to set others free as well – and they don't like it! Their trick is to cheat you and blur your vision, to tempt you to take part in a different story from the one you choose yourself. They prey on your time, your energy, your strength and your loot. And they will lure, tempt, threat, provoke and pull you, if you don't pay attention and stay on your course. Stay focused and keep your energy levels high, when you meet and face the demons. The more you let them prey on you, the more evil and powerful they become.

Level 6

You are well on your way to becoming an epic player in the Game of the Future. You have stepped out of your comfort zone and diverged from the safety of the tribal path of the past and are headed into the unknown. En route, you have lost your way and found yourself again.

Actually, it's not possible for you to find yourself if you haven't been lost.

On Level 6, you're now ready to take a new standpoint, conquer a new vantage point. It's a vantage point that isn't made up of fear, conflict and the eternal fight for survival. Instead, it is based on love, abundance, new communities and interconnectedness. From this prospect your world begins. That is, until it doesn't anymore and you can start all over and conquer a new.

Level 7

The distance between visualization and creation has never been shorter. And as a futurist you are able to see the future, challenge vantage points (your own and those of others) and create amazing new things and solutions.

In the past, people used visualization and creation to produce 'more,' finding a new market, beating the others or to become the greatest, the first or the most well-known. In the future, it is all about making something 'better.' It's about creating a game that everyone can win and no one loses.

When you have completed Level 7, you have created better options for everyone. You have played the game to improve it and on the way you have upgraded your skills and are now richer and freer. You are ready to play the game again with the sole purpose of getting more people to join the party.

The 'Modes' of the Game

You are not the first person in the history of mankind to attempt to complete and win the Game of the Future. Thousands of people before you have seen the future, created new rules and fought the battles that were important in their time.

The game has evolved from being rather primitive to becoming more and more sophisticated. In the first couple of rounds, our co-players were brutal cavemen, whom we had to convince that fire could be used the benefit of all. Later on, game changers fought regents and kings to make them treat their people right, just like our rebel ancestors paved the way for the welfare society, international cooperation, healthcare, proper working conditions, and much, much more. All the good things we have and know today happened because the futurists of the past spotted the future, believed in it and became the game changers that changed the rules of the game.

Make no mistake: It was always an uphill endeavor. They were killed, burned, expelled, ridiculed and rarely earned the recognition they so deserved while they lived. They are the ones, who often lose the battle but win the war, for the future will come whether we like it or not. And the future has always shed its love on rebels, futurists and game changers.

The time we live in now is perhaps the most epic era ever. The players of the past made it much more easy for you to complete all seven levels faster than ever before. Their results changed the rules for the better, which has made the game board much more diverse and civilized, but also more complex to navigate. We still see suffering, death, misery, wars and injustice in the world, and psychopaths, narcissists, sociopaths are still bulldozing and roaring ahead. But their ways have become less socially acceptable. The awareness has changed and when every now and then their scheme is revealed, the consequences are of a completely different scope and scale. The world has always been out of joint. The difference is that now we all more aware of it and still more and more people feel compelled to act.

The future is calling. And a new generation of players are waking up.

Some game changers were more revolutionizing than others. One example is the moon landing in 1969, where all of a sudden mankind was able to view the Earth from a completely different perspective. By a magic stroke, the game opened up and provided a new prospect as well as insight, a vantage point which had never been available before: our planet, Gaia, as seen from outer space, floating in the dark as a blue and beautiful ball so full of life.

A lot of the problems we face today can only be resolved from this vantage point. The climate crisis, wars, biodiversity, mental health, energy, poverty, sickness, quality of life, consumption, the good life, transportation, etc. No one person, country or defined territory can solve these issues on their own.

We can only do it if we work together. And only if we play to make everyone a winner and make sure no one loses.

So, you see why it's super important for you to choose the right mode to play?

The Two Modes You Can Play

TRIBAL VS. PLANETARY

Chapter 2
The Two Modes You Can Play

At this point, there are two different modes to play: 'Tribal' and 'Planetary' as coined by the American theoretical physicist and futurist, Michio Kaku. In theory, they are very different and distinct, but in practice, you'll find that you often get confused, because they somewhat overlap. You'll not be able to 'see' what to do, only 'feeling in your gut' will move you forward. You must be able to activate the energy source that is your 'belief' without being discouraged. It's a tough job being a pioneer, but luckily, it's also never been easier to hook up with kindred spirits.

Tribal [Unlocked]

Also known as the 'Classic mode,' where building a tribe of like-minded people and colonizing the world is on top of the agenda. In this mode, the players are concerned with creating a society, where people speak the same language and believe in more or less the same things. Players organize and play the well-known 'them vs. us'-game to fight each other off, and they are generally driven by greed, sex and fear, but also by love and passion – which often proves difficult to control, though. Their main concern is if they will run out of resources, which is why they seek to conquer, own and accumulate together.

In Tribal mode, players spend a lot of time and energy organizing teams whether it's in a family or a tribe of supporters for when the going gets tough. The game is all about establishing and drawing up boundaries, building businesses and institutions, controlling behavior, distributing resources and allocating goods and welfare to yourself, your friends, and those in need – that is if the earnings allow for it.

Success is achieved when the individual has found his or her shelf and role in society, owns a lot of stuff and cultivates the ability and maintains a moral and ethical incentive to share whatever is surplus with others. The tribal players' inherent dilemma is therefore the drive and wish to liberate some people, on the one hand, but they're only able to do so by exploiting or subduing other people on the other.

Historically, only a select few have had the surplus and status to actually win in the Tribal mode. And the white man has been the dominant player. But as the rules changed, more and more people moved up in Maslow's hierarchy of needs, which allowed a lot of new players (e.g. women and less pale men) to actually win in the Tribal mode.

And the most exciting thing…? It is now possible for those who'd rather play in another mode (or just grew tired of Tribal) to play the Planetary mode.

Planetary [Unlocked]

Also known as the 'Connected mode,' where the entire planet is connected across borders, cultures and belief systems. A global community of people working together with machines and artificial intelligence has seen the day of light.

Unlike in Tribal, the players in Planetary see themselves as part of a whole and they are less concerned with owning stuff as with having access to the things they need when they need it. The fear of lacking

resources has been replaced by the longing to get rid of one's ego, live one's full potential and make a positive difference for others.
In Planetary, players are in control of all types of energy and they invest themselves in solving problems locally and across borders. Success is about creating something that grows with the player, while making a positive difference in the world. The most important characteristics are visualization and creative powers as well as the selfless desire to watch other people unfold their potential on their own terms – with all the mistakes and hassle that follow.

Where players in Tribal argue and fall into trench warfare fighting the 'them vs. us'-fight on autopilot, Planetarians share the need to be sensitive, tolerant, empathetic and constructive. An approach which is not at all easy, because tribal players remain resolute and keep bulldozing as the charming and manipulative creatures they are. And so they can be extremely destructive, because their worst fear is to be stripped naked and lose face. They would rather die jumping off the burning building taking you with them in the fall than letting go of what they feel is their claim, the things that define them and the things they own. For this very reason they are at a standstill on the evolutionary 'Bildungsreise' of mankind. 'Homo ego' is the survivor. Certainly, big egos have also helped us move forward in previous times, but now their time is over. As Harvey Dent says to Batman, "You either die a hero, or you live long enough to see yourself become the villain."

The players in Planetary have to work together to create a new set of rules and rehearse habits that will triumph the laws of the jungle and its call for selfishness. And they will do so in a way that will promote listening and being open, which will make it an advantage to be vulnerable, sensitive, compassionate and full of love, kindness and good intentions.

At this stage, it's only possible to play Tribal or Planetary – which is also more than enough! But the Curious Georges amongst you might enjoy exploring the new modes that a collective 'pass' at Planetary will open up for the generations to come.

Stellar [Locked]

Also known as the 'Exploration mode,' where players have developed an interconnectedness at the other end of the spectre from the egotistical Tribal. They are ready to leave the planet, not because it's crashing or burning down, but because they are longing for something more. Longing for new adventures. Planet Earth has been saved and all is well, but the players are now eager to explore their prospects and experience the insight that makes great stories.

In Stellar, the players are not just physically and technologically connected. They also share a spiritual connection. This mode is not yet unlocked and so we don't really know much about it. Our guess is that the reason why so many people today are experiencing anxiety, unrest, depression and stress is not that they are broken. No, they are the 'mutants' of the future: Our children's brains are currently in the process of developing the ability to hold hyper complexity. One cause of apathy is hyperactive empathy. Super empaths can sense how others are doing and they can feel their feelings. The problems occur if they mistake the feelings of others as their own, which will result in super empaths shutting down or becoming strange, sick and embittered beings.

In Stellar, all players are empathetic and sensitive. So, if you and your kids are ahead of your time, you might experience some tough love in this transitional phase between Tribal and Planetary.

The Stellar mode will be unlocked when enough players have won and passed Planetary. Our 'guesstimate' is some time within the next 100-1,000 years.

Galactic [Locked]

– or the 'Final Quest mode.' In the Galactic mode, players must unite to pass the intergalactic IQ-test. Everybody has to join in and be successful. On all levels. For how can it be that we have not yet met any aliens, when all the smart people have agreed that life does exist on other planets? The answer: Frankly, because the aliens don't bother. If you were a sophisticated creature, hyper connected and full of love, would you feel up to meeting players that are still messing around in Tribal or have just taken their first baby steps into Planetary? Did aliens try to interfere with the game on other planets and discovered that the idea sucks? Probably. Are they placing quirky presidents in the United States and turning up the global temperature to propel the development forward? Maybe. Is the game of our life in fact their reality show? Most likely!

The Galactic mode will be unlocked when the players of Stellar have resolved all tasks on Planet Earth and in their immediate space front yard and when they have gained full insight. At this point, we've kind of run out of problems to solve and it's all become a little boring. We long to embark on new adventures – to infinity and beyond! If we manage the task in our very first attempt, it will happen in about 1,000-1,500 years from now, give and take.

But, if Tribal has a comeback and not enough gamers want to (or dare) play the Planetary mode, it might take much longer for us to get there.

And then there's a risk that we burn down the planet before we even get started. Meaning: Everybody loses and no one wins.

You Are a Great, Yet Fallible Person

If you are the same age as us, you might remember the time when you were playing the games of 'Pack Man,' 'Mission Impossible,' 'Donkey Kong' or 'Space Invaders.' If you are younger, your experiences with 'CounterStrike,' 'World of Warcraft' and 'Fortnite' are perhaps still fresh in your memory. The common denominator for all these games is that most likely, you didn't master the game the first time your hand grabbed that joypad. It was just fun! As in every other game, the road into the Game of the Future is paved with mistakes. In order to master the game, you need to go through what we call the 'stinking stage,' which is where you really get to know the game, where you experiment and put your ideas to the test and really, really, REALLY suck at it. You have to be able to stink in order to be great.

Before you find your way, you will get lost. Don't freak out about it. We moderns have to lose our way in order to be able to find ourselves. You must go astray and try what it feels like to have the wrong job, the wrong friends and making wrong decisions in order to figure out what you don't want. Before you decided to follow this path into the future, nobody had walked your future path. The road that everyone else is taking outside the game is wide, comfortable and safe and therefore also a little boring. Maybe it is not even yours?

Whether or not you need to find your way or if you are well on your way already, we want to turn up the heat in your engine. Because the future is now! The future is here, it's ready for you and you are able to reach out to people on the other side of the world via a broad selection of digital platforms that give you access to knowledge, counselling, funding and all the other resources you need. So why are you still hesitating?

Is something holding you back? Or not?

The brake is installed within you. On the one hand, the world is so complex that you have a hard time figuring it all out. Complexity is one of the greatest enemies of our time. It is so strong and overpowering that it catches up with human intelligence and makes us apathetic and comfort seeking, killing all incentives of development before we have even begun the work.

On the other hand, you might have pulled the brake because you are a sterling character. Kind people worry about other people, they want others to join the party and they don't like bulldozing or stepping on somebody's toes. And so they juuuust have to pack a lunch bag, take out an insurance and do a thousand other things before they embark on something new and potentially frightening

Good people (i.e. the ones, who just want to live a good life and help others as much as they can; people, who don't run their engines on bragging about riches and rising in the ranks) tend to play themselves small. It's easy to think that you are just a tiny human being in a very big world, and so what good will it do, if you take the lead? The thought alone gives you the fidgets. But worrying is just the flabbiest feeling in the universe. It's a privileged position that makes you highlight the right concerns and issues that you talk about with you friends, but which you never come around to take action on. You're thinking the right things, but you don't walk the talk, because you think you need an encyclopedic understanding of the world first. Or that you need permission.

It is as if your life is a game of Parcheesi and you have been sent to the nest and now have to wait until you roll a six to move on with your life.

Don't do that! For, if good people don't step up and break the rules of the game to seize the future, the opportunists will take over. They are the coxcombs with broken morals, big egos and no ethical compass, and they will have free rein to start wars, create crises, fuck up the economy, the environment, the institutions, the workplaces, social media and the technological development.

Good people don't like calling others evil. Evil becomes an illness, a trauma, something they can't help. Again, it becomes an excuse to avoid stepping up and find your place in the game, conquering your vantage point, and standing your ground. So, consider this question: Do you want to live in a world of coxcombs? No, the hell you don't! In the Game of the Future, you are allowed to be angry. We bet you can make a long list of things big and small that you think are not good enough and which you are willing to fight to change.

Bringing your anger and the feeling of being stepped on by opportunists with you into the game will put you in a better position to find your way, because you have already defined what is right and wrong to you. The fight of 'good vs. evil' is an epic battle which has been fought since forever. And it has never been more relevant. The world doesn't change by making observations, analyszing and putting on a creased, worried face. It changes when good people like yourself take your seat at the table and become a part of the game.

Historically, the world changes very fast, when the good guys fight for their magic visions. And when those visions become the reality, humanity as a whole gains more riches, freedom and happiness.

In the Game of the Future, good people should earn good money. You don't need to live the life of a martyr or play the role of the victim. You must be happy and live your most optimal life. In the future, money and technology are nothing but tools that boost what is already there. If you are good and gain access to a lot of money, you will only do more good. If, on the other hand, you are a douchebag, well… you know how that ends.

The opportunists are already playing the Game of the Future. And they will win if you don't do anything.

So, dear futurist, gamer of the future … Are you ready?

Now is the time to put down the book, because in a little while, you are going to cross the Rubicon. And then you will be hooked.

One thing is fore sure: it can very well be the most terrific, dramatic and uncomfortable game of your life! But don't worry, we are your unwavering sidekick and we'll be here by your side and guide you on your journey.

But first, a warning.

Magic Moments

The game will provide a bunch of opportunities for you to earn a shit load of money, experience new things and solve important problems. But as in any other game, there is no guarantee that things will turn out as you expect. The future in itself is not a promise of justice. The justice we enjoy on a daily basis is only effectuated because good people get out of bed every day and uphold it with their words and actions.

So, when we say that the game can upgrade your skills and make you richer and freer, it can happen in a myriad of different ways.

The definition of wealth is 'to have access to' – clean drinking water, opportunities, traveling, friendships, love, knowledge, decision makers and much more.

Economic wealth is just one way (and sometimes a poor way) of being rich. Focus on what you want to achieve with your wealth and the things you get access to. You will realize things about yourself that will make you change your path in life and your strategy. The Game of the Future makes it easier for you to make your own decisions rather than the ones dictated by society, your parents, your boss and everyone else. This is freedom. Being able to be at peace with your own choices.

But freedom is not always fun, nor is it always very comfortable. You will need friends. Robin Hood probably froze his ass off in the Sherwood Forest, but he did have his merry men (and women) to back him up and support him.

This game will make it clear to you that something needs to be sorted and dropped. Something you simply can't do anymore. Would you be willing to give up some of your comforts (the couch, your status, your position in society) for freedom? For the future? For the other players?

What we can guarantee is skill and competence. Just like a computer game, there will be setbacks, wrong turns, doubts and frustrations.

You will stumble upon trolls and demons, and separate friends from enemies, but you will also experience the rush of having cracked the code and mastering the game to move up in levels.

This rush is what we call magic moments.

Through magic moments you will discover your magic, and the irritation that follows, and when you find a way to bear this, there really is no limitation as to what you can achieve and accomplish.

Your Mission Should You Choose to Accept

And now to your mission. We want to send you off into the game to build the bridge from Tribal to Planetary and make sure that Planetary will flourish and appear much more attractive to the new generations of players. We want to make a futurist out of you – a very special gamer with the qualities to not just move yourself, but to move others. Together with us at Universal Futurist and everyone else we meet on our way, say: "Yes, yes, yes, I want in, too!" Together we can be a global movement, a fellowships of futurists. Powered, not by violence, power, fear or anxiety, but by vision, hope, community, love, kindness and trust.

Win the future with vision, hope, community, love, kindness and trust.

At this point in time, world history is balancing on the verge of Planetary. So much is at stake, because we both have the means and opportunities to take ourselves to the next level as well as destroying the entire planet.

Climate change, overpopulation, lack of resources, the automatization that threatens to change the labor market making millions of people dispensable, the fear of artificial intelligence, fake news, refugees, and fanatics. All these challenges are Tribal-made and can only be resolved in the Planetary mode.
Expect to meet players, who don't want to move on to the Planetary

mode. These are players, who fight fiercely to maintain the status quo so that they can satisfy their need for power and profit. Maybe you already know who your enemies are? And maybe you can already lower your weapons and minimize the time spent on fighting old battles and instead turn toward to future and prioritize all that is new, fun exciting and adding value?
This is the challenge of our time.

This is the fight you've been chosen to fight.

And we will do all we can to help you succeed.

Together with all the other players, who want to play the Planetary mode.

Hack the Game of the Future

Since we are on the verge of Planetary, there are still a lot of things we don't know. And as a pioneer, you need to pitch in to make the rules.

As the Gandalf we're trying to be, we want to give you some assets for your backpack that will increase your chances of getting success and winning the game.

The game of the future is hyper complex and hyper connected. There is not one single education that will give you all the tools you need. What's more important is to stay in the zone of curiosity and naivety rather than insisting on being wise and blind on experience. You can spend five years in therapy trying to understand why you had a bad childhood. Unfortunately, these sessions will not provide the recipe for a great life as an adult.

You can be well-read and highly educated, but it's not mandatory. Since the Game of the Future is hyper complex, the amount of information will always exceed your comprehension and mental capacity. If you're finding that you're incapable of making a decision, all you need to do is meeting the world with a neutral and open "well, well" or "aha."

The future is hyper connected, which means that everything you need is already out there. And the more you can set the pace yourself, the easier you can be found. Your magic will resonate with the world. And if you think you're stupid, we'll say that it's a great starting point.

When we travel into the unknown, we are always sensuously guided by our gut feeling. You must be able to see, feel and believe in the future. And then, when you've gained the insight and conquered your vantage point, you will know if it's important to you.

Look for the Magic Moments

In Tribal, all players are gold diggers. In Planetary, you must look for magic. Your magic moments, whether big or small, are like shining gems placed to lead you on the right path. You will code your player to choose the right path by experiencing magic moments, taking a break with them and getting to know them, so that they can recharge your batteries and help you reach 100%. Every day!

However, in spite of the magic, the future will also be a source of irritation no matter what you do. The difference is that when you play in the Tribal mode, the irritation wears you down. In Planetary, it's your new best friend. Irritation is the surrounding environment trying to get into transformative contact with you – admittedly in a really socially handicapped way. If the universe is calling you, pick up the phone. If you don't, it will knock on your door. And if you still don't answer, in the end, you will get a massive wake-up call.

Which is why you really should look for irritation, too. Tell yourself that when something or someone annoys the shit out of you, it's because they are right. Don't plant a tribal ax between their brows. Take a deep breath instead and ask what it is that you don't want to hear. It's only hard the first 28,789 times.

Remember that if you choose to stay put in the pleasant and comfortable well-known, and if you fly into a rage and immediately attack whenever someone confronts you, you are – per definition – playing in the Tribal mode.

Buddy Up and Pledge Allegiance to a New Type of Community

You just can't win the Planetary mode alone. Your most important trends are often found in your blind spot, which is why you need someone to help you out. It's a technique that we call blind spotting.

A part of the game is to inspire others to get on board and create new and strong communities that will change the world. In Tribal, we were playing with people who for the most part looked a lot like ourselves. But since the future is multi-cultural and works across borders, you will want a whole lot of buddies, preferably a crowd of people unlike yourself.

Your buddy has your back and wants what's best for you, even though that means you'll annoy one another. Your buddy will love to act the part.

The Game of the Future is fun. And dangerous. And you will not make it on your own, and if you did, it would be really boring.

Look at it from the perspective of the diver. No diver would dream of diving into the big blue ocean alone without a buddy. Your buddy double checks your gear, points at the funny fish, keeps an eye on sharks and makes sure that you get back to the boat in one piece. And you will do the same for your buddy.

As you move further into the unknown parts of the game, you will need people that see the world from a different perspective than you. People with whom you can create a dedicated and pledging community. You must establish a training relation, where you love to watch each other fail and evolve.

You buddy was your pal in kindergarten, who held your hand in the row of twos. Everybody needs a buddy. A partner, who has your back, holds you responsible, keeps you on track, annoys you and says the things that you don't want to hear. It is a person, who will also share your excitement when you succeed and your magic moments.

Your buddy is not necessarily someone you know well, and it definitely doesn't have to be someone you agree with. Your buddy's job is to help you look around the corner, challenge your taboos and make you take a closer look at your blind spots. Your buddy provokes you to do a little better and help you let go of old ideas and convictions by pushing you out of your comfort zone. A mentor is on a higher level than you, but your buddy is your equal and you sincerely want to raise each other up.

Your buddy is the beginning of the pledging community of diverse buddy relations that can mix and mingle across the world. These are the indispensable communities of the future and they are characterized primarily by two things:

1. We appreciate each other just as we are.

2. Long, healthy and some times conflict-ridden relations.

The new communities are crucial if we want to unfold the Planetary mode. You need to feel safe and appreciated by other talented people in dedicated communities that cultivates the ability to unlearn in order to learn again. The job is not to reach the goal or 'to produce' as much as it is about becoming 'what the world needs' and appropriating wicked skills while having fun.
If you prefer to play the Game of the Future on your own, you should at least invite a couple of imaginary buddies to accompany you, maybe even some well-known visionary buddies from history? We do recommend living human beings though as they are usually the most annoying. So, buddy up!

When you've found your buddy (and you are more than welcome
to carry a bunch), we will invite you to recite the Holy Buddy Oath
together:

"My buddy is my friend. I promise to help, train and push you,
motivate and annoy you to play the Game of the Future and change
the rules of the game for the better. And you, my buddy, will do the
same for me. We will train the skills and competencies that we don't
yet have, but which we can see are crucial for being successful in the
future we want to see. We will begin today, and we will spot trends
every day, even if it's only for 30 seconds. I pledge to be your buddy,
also when I don't have the time or when I don't like to be hard on you.
For it is in my game and in my buddy's that I wish for us to win.

After ___ days, we will celebrate our successes by/with:

____

Signed (me):

____

Signed (my buddy):

____

Prepare for Pain, Distress, Loneliness and Misery

Most gamers go through Planetary in three phases. Some gamers are free from the beginning, while others are tied to others or other things by force, habit or choice.

In order to complete Planetary, the players must emancipate and become independent, which some will experience as a smooth operation, while others will experience it as traumatizing. But you have to experience the existential crisis that follows taking responsibility for yourself before your can step back into the community and the interconnectedness.

Not out of fear, seeking comfort, an increase of salary or out of worry, but because we believe in each other and want to give more than we expect to receive in return.

As player, you need to be able to control your emotions and our thoughts. Picture this: You're standing on a railway station. When the train comes in and wants you to board, you can choose to let the train go by if you know with yourself that it won't take you somewhere nice or interesting.

Feelings are fart. Everyone likes their own better. That's totally natural, but we have to stop revelling in them. The farts. Go outside instead and feel the fresh air of the future. Feel your feelings, but don't indulge in them. Cough them up like a cat coughs up hair balls and explore them curiously. In the back of this book, you will find an Emotional Encyclopedia to look up the feelings and emotions that you can to use to make an impact, instead of, like in Tribal, leaving them inside of you and, as a consequence, burning out.

Tell Stories

People who don't own their story will merely react to what is happening. People who on the other hand know how to weave the pieces of the future into the red thread that makes an intriguing patchwork story about you, me and everyone else will gain momentum to change the rules of the game. Stories that create fear will maintain us in the Tribal mode. Stories that open up the world and create hope will set us free in Planetary.

This is why stories are the most powerful tool at your disposal.

As a futurist, you will be able to give a lot of people better tools to design and narrate their own stories. They will star in their own version of the Game of the Future, so they too can find a way to change the rules of the game and become game changers themselves.

So, take out your dust brush and dust off the old stories, so you can replace them with new and exciting ones that reflect the challenges we're currently facing.

Making up something new can be very abstract, while quitting something can be very tangible. Cleaning up and saying goodbye will however set you free.

The so-called 'enlightened people' typically find it easy to look down upon the mob messing about with their sex, drugs and rock 'n roll behavior. Why don't they just quit and read a book? But remember that if you create a new team of good and enlightened people vs. those who you think are stupid and selfish, you're still playing in the Tribal mode yourself. So, get your own house sorted first, make peace with your own mistakes and be the change you want to see.

They say that Hell doesn't allow forgiveness.

True, we've all made mistakes, hurt other people and we all live with grief and disappointment. We are just imperfect creatures making our way as good as we can.

Know that when you step into the Game of the Future, you're starting with a clean slate.

You are forgiven.

Look ahead instead, for in front of you lies a world of opportunities, the possibility of hitting it big and contributing to creating a future in which everyone can win at the expense of no one.

We believe in you!

So, futurist and future game changer, may the force of the future be with you!

FROM MORE TO BETTER

TUTORIAL

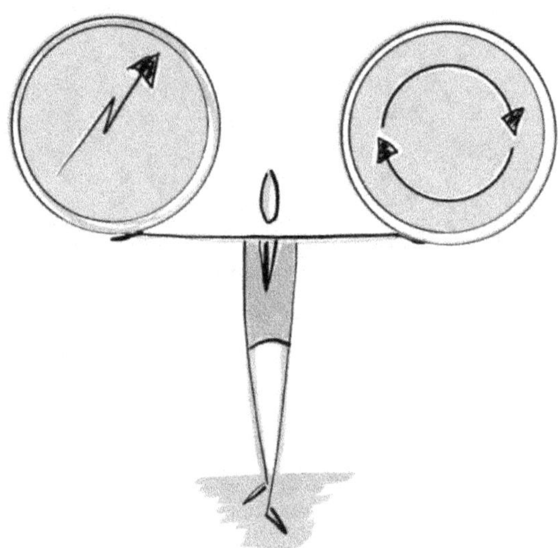

Chapter 3
Tutorial
From more to better

If we were you, at this point, we would think: "Okay, enough already with all the words, let's get this ball rollin'." Okay, sorry! You're right.

The easiest and most simple way to get the Game of the Future going in the Planetary mode is to use the trend "from 'more' to 'better'" as your game changer.

If at one point you get stuck, get busy or become confused, stop and think: "Is this 'more' or is this 'better'?"

Later on in the book, we will dig deeper into the ways in which you can find your personal game changer. All you need to know at this stage is that a game changer is the trend that makes the future zoom in on you. It's that moment when you realize that if this happens, it will completely change the rules of the game for me.

Now, in this tutorial, you're using your borrowed game changer to practice thinking: "Is this more or better? Do you need 'more coffee' or 'better coffee?' Is a 'bigger fridge' going to make you happy or will it just provide 'more space' to make a mess in? Will 'more likes' on social media get you there, or do you need something 'better?'"

The question is, what does 'better' really mean? We are not going to give you the answer, because that is the whole point. This is what you need to figure out for yourself. Hahah! So contemplate this: When or where in your life is something, not right or wrong, but 'better,' to you?

Tribal mode is a lot like a game of Monopoly, which is definitely not about 'better.' The game board is locked. The lines have been drawn and there's only one direction you can go: round and round and round and round – no vision what so ever in sight. You can't just take off and build a house on a property outside the board. If someones stops to ask where we're headed, we'll say: "Ehm, I don't know, but we have to keep the wheel spinning!" Round and round and round. In Monopoly, success means buying properties, building a shit load of plastic and then charge your friends the highest possible rent, which means that in the end, they'll go bankrupt. You win in Monopoly, when you're all high and mighty sitting all alone (and together with the bank) in you plastic palace, while everyone else left because they think you're a huge douchebag. So, congratulations!

Monopoly is not a game that brings out the best of us. Several attempts have been made to give one player an advantage: two dices to roll instead of one, and whenever the player wins money, the bank will double the profit. Time and time again, the same story plays out. People transform their Dr. Jekyll self into a nasty Mr. Hyde persona. They become assholes, frankly, moving their fucking car around the board while gloating and mocking the others, who are now poor as church mice. Afterward, the winner is then asked to reflect why they won the game, they'll highlight their strategic superiority. The fact that they had a huge advantage from the very beginning is never even mentioned.

The problem with Monopoly is that it is fundamentally a game that a lot of people need to lose so that a few can win. The game is built on scarcity, conflict and stupid rules that bring out the absolute worst in us. And this was in fact the very intention of the game to begin with as it was created by a teacher who wanted to exemplify the pointless and fallible nature of capitalism.
So, whenever you feel disappointed on behalf of humanity, remind yourself that it's because we're playing the wrong game. A game that brings out the worst in us.

A game that is coming to an end.

The planetary Game of the Future is completely different, thank god! This game compares to a computer game, where you're figuring out the rules as you play along. You experiment and you learn, and if you die, you just start over again. You'll ask other players how they fought the trolls and how they managed to vanquish the obstacles, and you know that moving up in levels will not happen until you've completed the tasks and the challenges of your current level. Unlike Monopoly, the Game of the Future wants you to win for being you and not on account of impersonating some inflexible and furtive character.

Once Upon a Time

All great fairy tales begins with 'Once upon a time…' In Tribal, it's the same, for it once was a fairy tale. In hunting for a better life, 'more' was actually better. If you don't have food on the table and you then get some, you will be satisfied. If you don't have a chest freezer and then you get one, happiness is on! If you only have your two legs for walking and you get a bicycle, the world opens up. This is still how it is in many places of the world.
But the world is changing. We don't want 'more' bicycles, we want a 'better' bicycle. The Norwegians, for instance, find is funny that the best-selling bicycle in Denmark is the mountain bike.

A long life is not the same as a great life. Growth is not automatically creating welfare. And a lot of the problems the world is facing today will not be resolved by saving up or doing more or less of the things we already do. A bigger military force will not annihilate terrorism in itself. Less productivity will not resolve the climate crisis. Higher wages won't make nurses happier at work. A pork sausage will not be ten times as delicious by being ten times as long or ten times as expensive.

If you had to choose, what do you really need? 'More' programs on TV or 'better' programs? 'More' politicians or 'better' politicians? 'More' leadership or 'better' leadership? 'More' rules' or 'better' rules? 'More' food or 'better' food?
'More' is easy, it only takes duplication and scaling. And we'll turn

the lever up and down. There are areas where this maneuver is still working for the better, but there really is a limit as to how many cost-saving reforms the health care system can take or how fast industrial workers can run. Transportation is another great example. Today, driving through London takes longer that before the car was invented.

Think Differently

'Better' is an altogether different way of thinking. It takes time, patience, deep thinking and reflection. And it takes courage to become aware and then actively choosing to take the road less traveled or simply treading the path yourself. In a future where so many new things will happen, we can no longer lean on history. We need to be able to stand tall and create something that's never been seen before. Something better seen from our perspective, from our point in time.

But what exactly does 'better' mean?

In Tribal mode, for instance, we look at the labor market and think that 'more work' is the best solution. Work, work, work your asses out, god damnit! In Tribal, the mantra is this: "If it worked in the old days, it's probably going to work fine tomorrow as well." So we decide that we need people to stay in the work force longer and preferably, they should not mess about as much in the early stages of their career. We'll prolong the retirement age and frown upon those, who don't work, and still, we view work as a punishment or a sort of military service that we want out of as fast as possible.

In Planetary, things look very different. We'll ask, "How can we create a labor market where we actually need one another? Where we develop and get better and more talented because it has value in itself?" We'll organize in a manner that's more free. And instead of retirement, we'll take breaks throughout life, we'll take on several employments and have a rich, local community life, and we'll view work as that place where we contribute our creative powers to make ourselves and others happy.

Cultivate Yourself Like a Plant

A great way to think about the shift from 'more' to 'better' is to view the things you want to create like a plant. In order to grow and thrive, the plant needs water, nutrients, sun and CO2. The limitation is always the thing that is lacking. So, if the plant needs water and you pour some water, the flowers will blossom until they reach the next limiting factor.

In Tribal, bigger yields were made by pouring more and more and more. Hunting for 'more' allowed the previous and the current generations to pass on the bill to the surrounding world, the climate and the future generations. If the old industries took account of those costs, none of them would generate profit. At all.

Planetary takes a holistic approach. 'More' is sometimes (but not always) the limiting factor. The task is to break with the more/less mindset and instead create something 'better' for more people (and the planet) using the right resources.

Expect that you already have the things you need to succeed. Choose to believe in it, feel it and get ready to see it and put them action.

Notice the point where the 'more'-mindset gets dangerous. If a plant gets too much water, you'll drown it. The same goes for sunlight, it only works till it doesn't work anymore. And the amount that's suitable for a pineapple will not do for a mushroom. Some people thrive with 'more,' 'faster' and 'taller,' while others suffers from stress or lose their motivation under these conditions.

'Better' requires us to read what the world needs and that we think hard and shake the bag to prescribe the things we have in the right amounts for the right target group to get the effect we want. And should we fail, we'll learn from the experience and try again.
One small step in a better direction is all the world needs.

More Gynecology or Better Gynecology?

Three months after a great talk in front of an international group of gynecologists in Germany (a group that we labeled 'people with warm hearts and cold hands'), we received an e-mail from one of the participants.

He wrote to say that he had thought long and hard about one of the questions we had asked: "What is better gynecology to you?" He also wrote that the question had hit a nerve in him and that it had hurt that he hadn't been able to answer the question right away.

So, with the question and the reflections in mind, he had turned down an offer of becoming a partner in a fancy practice, which in itself was a great deal, because where he came from this position signalled status and high standing in the community. But he simply couldn't feel the magic, "My soul wasn't in it," he wrote.

Instead he had invested in a bus and decorated it IKEA-style to realize his dream of bringing the gynecologist to the people, who needed him the most, the women who would never go to a fancy clinic on a high-end street, and for whom he was so passionate about making a difference.

'More' is either or and 'better' is yes and no. For in the future you can do it all: be happy, healthy, talented and competent, free, rich, have great friends, time for your family, sleep well at night and do great things for the community and the planet. Things are not mutually exclusive. You can in fact have it all.

All you have to do is to be willing to break the rules and make magic from whatever it is 'better' means to you.
The Danish philosopher, Søren Kierkegaard, once said that music has to resonate with you in order for you to truly appreciate it. And it is this internal resonator you should rehearse, so you can feel the music swinging your vibe.
'Better' is a muscle you can train, so do it as often as possible. Don't

drink more coffee, drink 'better' coffee. Don't have more meetings, have 'better' meetings. Don't work out more, do it 'better.' Ask others what 'better' means to them.

And listen loud, keep an open mind. If you don't know the answer immediately, so what!? When you think about it, it's kind of exciting, isn't it? Be curious about who you are. And you will be well on our way.

Sometimes, 'More' Is Definitely Not 'Better'

In 2018, one of the biggest investment banks in the world, Goldman Sachs, was not well on their way. In 2018, they gave a recommendation that clients and customers shouldn't invest in gene therapy. The reason? They didn't believe in the sustainability of a business model that actually cures diseases and restores people to health.

Yup, you heard that right! Healthy people is not a sustainable business model. Or, in other words: You can't make money on people, who are well and healthy. Only people who are sick will get your cashflow running – especially those who are suffering from a long-term illness, now that's good business – thank you very much!

Goldman Sachs is one of four examples of how players in our time think.

Their case clearly shows how the tribal view of healthcare simply doesn't hold water anymore. And as long as this mindset of making a profit on sickness is the fundamental principle in the health care sector, we're all caught in the more/less death loop of doom.

Are the tribal rich taking the lion's share? Yup! Are there few winners and a lot of losers? Oh, yes! Does the world need 'Big Pharma' to star in the movie about the future? Definitely no!

Luckily, there are other players in strategic positions in place in other companies. The new players are waking up to realize that they should create a new (and better) business model that generates a profit on curing diseases and restoring people to good health. In 2019, Ernest & Young, one of the biggest accounting and consultancy firms in the world with 247,570 employees and activities in more than 150 countries, made this vision their strategic bet for the future: Breaking down the old rules and re-create a better, global and more sustainable healthcare system with many new and better vantage points to conquer.

A Better War

The employees at Ernest & Young are not the only ones focusing on 'better' instead of 'more.' It might sound a bit off at first, but in the military, 'better war' actually makes sense. 'More war' is to win the war, whereas 'better war' is to win the peace.

Winning a war can leave a country completely devastated and smashed to pieces, so when the victor wants to win the peace, the armed forces will have to secure law and order for the rebuilding process, which requires a completely different training and mentality. In 'better war,' the military doesn't make use of land mines, because the mines prolong the war into the future. Denmark, for example, wasn't declared clear of the land mines laid out in World Word II before 2012, and in England, they still discover bombs that were dropped during the Battle of England.

For years, the American military has been working quietly behind the scenes on a green transition, primary for two reasons:

- They predict that the climate challenge will amplify all existing conflicts.
- If you get rid of old energy and transform into a strong, green and more intelligent supply chain, you are strategically in a stronger position and ahead of the game.

Among other things, the American forces are currently developing ships that use sea water as a source of energy and their elite troops are already indefinitely self-sufficient on energy.

'Better war' is a great example of how players can move into the Planetary mode without following their heart. The motivation here is not to be 'better' human beings as much as it is a need to conquer a better vantage point, from where you can uphold and renew the position you want to maintain. The incentive is still to win Tribal-style, but if they were to play the Game of the Future by the old rules only, they would lose both games.

Do Better And Pay It Forward

The true winners of the Game of the Future are, perhaps unexpectedly, found in the industries of the warm and semi-warm hands.

Educators and CSOs (Community Service Officers) are some of the only clients to call in advance before workshops and events to ask us if they should bring a lunch bag. How typical and telling that those who give the most to the world are the ones who expect to get the least in return. They also typically open the lid on empty coffee pots to let the staff know which pots need a refill. In a quick comparison of industries, it's a safe bet that coffee mugs and pots are left all over the room, behind curtains, on the bathroom, under the chairs, whenever clients from the financial sector come to visit. The littlest things in your behavior can say quite a lot about who you are in the world. You can also tell by the way a person's position in society allows them to act in a certain way. And then the never-ending challenge of turning down the volume on the spoiled ego and move on 'from entitlement to enlightened.'

Educators, social workers and CSOs are hands down among the sweetest and nicest, most self-sacrificing human beings in this world. They don't just think in 'better,' they also care about passing on this mindset: "How can I make life a little bit better for those who come after me (if only to get a coffee refill a little faster)?"

A lot of these people are born Planetarians, and for years on end they've personally as well as professionally fought to create a new set of rules. Every day they wipe away the snot off the noses of ungrateful kids. They pick up drunkards in the streets and fight the good fight for vulnerable people they don't even know or are related to. From early morning to late at night.

In Tribal, people who don't have a place in society are generally annoying. When you fall through the social safety net and hit rock bottom, it is difficult to rise and get back on your feet. From their perspective, the future looks pretty dark: the rich and healthy are getting better and better, while sick, poor and vulnerable people are getting worse.

Imagine a classroom of eight children and three adults. Does that sound crazy? Not in Planetary, where it's considered completely normal for people to take precedence over the system. In Tribal, it's the other way around. Here, budgets determine that it can't be done, because it's not affordable.

From the planetary perspective, the outlook makes us ask what our treatments of our fellow human beings says about who we are in the world, if we do this or that? Ugh. The minute we ask this question, planetary players will wire more money, send more resources and set up a 24hour support group.

For, in the Planetary mode, we all help each other out, so that everyone wins and no one looses.

So, dear friend! Where are you already doing better?

Where are you already making decisions based on who you want to be in the world?

Take you experience and magic moments from this place and make it better.

Not more, but 'better.'

This will get the ball rolling. Do it every day for the rest of your life and the rest will follow.

If you make this pledge, you can quit with a clear conscience and close the book now.

If, however, you're hungry for more and your calling is big, then read on and let's take a closer look at the two modes, Tribal and Planetary, so you can see for yourself how much is at stake, how your brain is in fact cheating you, and how you can invite everyone else to join the party.

Are you ready for the next level?

Level 1

FROM MBA TO MBS

HOW TO WAKE UP YOUR FUTURE SENSE AND FIND YOUR WAY ON THE PLANETARY GAME BOARD

Hey!

Chapter 4
From MBA to MBS

There was a time when having an MBA (Master of Business Administration) listed on your résumé was an entry ticket to being promoted and gaining status in the business community as well as a more than comfortable amount of money in the bank.

For those of you thinking, "Huh?", an MBA is an expensive and time consuming management degree, an Ironman for business people, you might say. Through time, the MBAs have served the tribal kings of Monopoly well.

But those days are over.

In the future, visionaries and empathetic people, who are willing to take a risk, become the important players. To all of us. Totally cool if you do have an MBA in the bag, but you will need to upgrade it with ethics, courage and a sense of the future. If you think of the MBA as a watch, then the MBS is your compass. Where the watch represents management of the exterior, the compass represents your inner navigation tool.

If you want to do well in the future, you will need these essential qualities:

- The ability to hold on to yourself and refrain from acting the part of a wretched handyman serving single-minded bulldozing leaders or some outdated paradigm.

- The ability to see and identify connections in complex environments, being able to take it in and ask great questions.
- Creating fellowship in groups consisting of many different people.
- Creating the conditions that release potential.
- Knowing your own shadows and limitations and making peace with them.
- Showing compassion and the ability to put yourself in the shoes of others.
- Removing or destroying what's no longer needed.
- Being brave.
- Taking time off, resting and daydreaming.
- Being a pioneer for something to believe in, including standing up for moral and ethical principles and behavior.
- Looking out for the people and things you are responsible for.
- The ability to think for yourself. And thinking big, too.

We call the people who possess these qualities 'visionaries' or 'game changers'. And then we put them on a pedestal. Think about Apple's once so famous and very futuristic "Think Different"-campaign, in which the voice of the American actor, Richard Dreyfuss, accompanied a series of black and white pictures of icons like Bob Dylan, John Lennon and Martin Luther King, says:

Here's to the crazy ones. The misfits. The rebels. The troublemakers. The round pegs in the square holes. The ones who see things differently. They're not fond of rules. And they have no respect for the status quo. You can quote them, disagree with them, glorify or vilify them. About the only thing you can't do is ignore them. Because they change things. They push the human race forward. And while some may see them as the crazy ones, we see genius. Because the people who are crazy enough to think they can change the world, are the ones who do.

Nice one!

But you know… Geniuses live in the same world as you and me. They are not super human, they're just really good at seeing things that other people are not yet aware of. In their everyday life, they've developed a way of thinking in which they unconsciously collect trends as if they were pieces in a puzzle and then slowly piece them together into a new and bigger picture.

An idea they can act on and take to the next level!

The decisions they make are based on the trends that they spot and on new knowledge, which they then combine with their intuition and gut feeling.

In other words, they combine visualization and creative powers. And here's what's really cool: You can easily acquire the same sense of the future as these visionary game changers.

You don't need an MBA, you need an MBS (Mind, Body and Soul).

In order to move on to the next level, you have to internalize the habit of activating your MBS and the accompanying sense of the future. In the old days, storing your heart and soul in the trunk at the back of the car and only using reason as a basis for making decisions was perfectly normal. In hindsight, we often realize that it might not have been the best thing to do after all.

So, an MBS… Does it sound difficult? The good news is that you've already got it. And you have already passed! You were born with the MBS and throughout the years, you just forgot to train and rehearse it. So, that is what we'll do.

Use Your Three Brains

Tribal players typically only use one brain, the tribal brain. We'll take a closer look at it in the next chapter, for in the Game of the Future, being able to see, feel and predict the thought habits of the tribal brain is an asset, because you'll be able to make an active choice to activate your planetary brain and motivate others to cross the bridge to the future with you.

As a planetary player, you have access to these three brains:

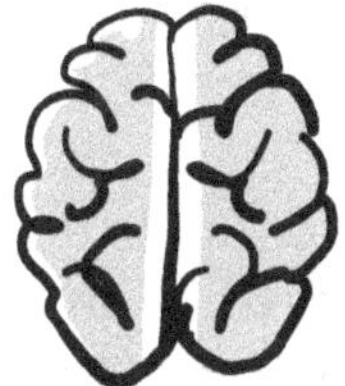 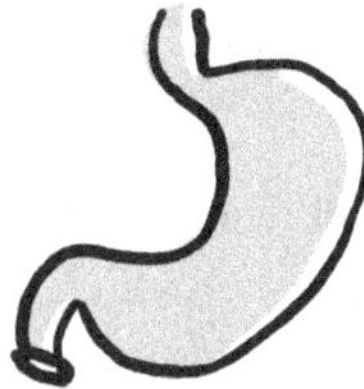 

Mind:
The rational brain
that sees the future.

Body:
The sensuous brain
that feels the future

Soul:
The spiritual brain that
believes in the future.

If you haven't learned how to use these three brains, it will create a clutter. Our reasoning says one thing, our body something else and the soul will point you in an entirely different direction. In this way, you'll easily develop a routine of excessive thinking, gather a choir of voices in your head. which will result in a cuckoo mind that will make you doubt if all your screws are fastened and well in place.

Since the beginning of time, visionary futurists and game changers have developed and improved the game using all three brains to their advantage. In the 1960s, the biologist Rachel Carson saw how rivers burst into flames due to chemical spills and she also sensed a decline in birds calling in the woods. Her books helped pave the way for the green movement, including the fight for pesticides. Facts and statistics can never stand alone. Seeing the future and choosing to go all-in to change the rules of the game is a full body experience.
So, let's take a look at how you take charge of your three brains – and wake up your MBS.

From the Head to the Entire Body

The soul, your spiritual brain, is eternal and perfect, but right now it takes up residence in your bodily meat truck on Planet Earth.

The soul carries your life purpose, your calling. It is made up of pure energy and relation, it's hyper complex and hyper connected. Where Tribal is about finding your place and playing a role, the Planetary mode will expose who you are already.

In your everyday life, your soul will feel like your intuition or everything that feels good and right, but which you can't really explain. We like using the word 'magic' for the mysterious part of you that is capable of doing and creating something that technology can't. Something we couldn't predict or explain, like the fact that Mozart at the age of five was able to play the piano better than any adult and that we still appreciate his music all around the world – that's pretty magic.

In the same way, things will never play out well if you don't do them wholeheartedly. When you carry your soul with you, the limit as to what you can achieve and accomplish practically doesn't exist.

In the old days, people believed that the brain (understood as the 86 billion nerve cells connected in a grey lump) was confined to the skull. But now we know that the brain sits in the whole body: the big one in the head, a smaller one in the heart and one in the stomach. We've all experienced pain to the heart and know what our gut feeling feels like. From now on, you wake up your future sense when you stop and listen to the signals from all of your three brains.

Maybe our descendants will look back at us and think we were strange because we limited ourselves to believe that the 'homo sapiens' is either a logical, reasonable and rational being or passionate and impulse-driven. Perhaps the primary reason that so many of us feel challenged by robots and algorithms is that we live our lives in our heads in a delimited department even, where focus is only on what can be weighed and measured. We are so much more than that.

The World Economic Forum has made the whole world talk about the fourth industrial revolution. And so most people like to think that the next revolution will be the fifth industrial revolution. But have you ever played with the idea that it might not come after all? Maybe something radically different will come instead. Not an industrial revolution per se, but a spiritual revolution that allows the heart and soul to join the party. Why? Because we need a better direction and something new to believe in, new and far more constructive and intelligent communities, because we long to feel, sense and experience things rather than just seeing them. The technological breakthroughs set us free to pursue other projects and capabilities, and because the 'free hand of capitalism' is an invisible force that drives the development in a certain direction, we need a GPS that is better and more value-based. Logical thinking is important, but we can't just extend these boards into the future. We also need to be able to imagine things, to make quantum leaps, and open up to see the wholeness and connect the dots in designing solutions, which, supported by Virtual Reality, might help us see the consequences of the things we are imagining.

People seem to thrive better, when emotions flow more freely and when we meet each other with empathy and experience a connection to others in love and friendships. When we find meaning and have something to fight for – when magic is allowed the space it deserves.

What Can You Do?

Practice using the brains you usually activate the least. If you think too much, try and be more spontaneous. If you respond primarily to your heart and gut feeling, then try listening a little louder to reason. It's not an either or-situation, but a question of yes and no. If you run from irritation and frustration, have the courage to stop and get the soul onboard. The soul speaks in whispers and it likes to take a break.

Informed guessing is also a great approach. When you're guessing, you're activating your MBS instead of trying to figure things out logically.

- How much spaghetti should I cook for seven people?

- How long does it take to drive from New York to Boston the day before Christmas Eve?
- How many breaks will we need en route?

If you're good at guessing, you're not a calculator providing an exact answer. You're providing a meaningful answer adjusted according to the circumstances.

You have to get your hands dirty, touch stuff and feel it on your own body. Of course, you can have an intellectual understanding of the technological prospects of self-driving cars.

But you have to feel it yourself.

So, go for a ride with your mother. Watch videos of others doing the same. Stay in tune with your gut feeling and listen to what your heart has to tell you about the dilemmas that self-driving cars create.

- What is good and bad?
- To whom?
- What do we want to do while we're in them?
- Is there a steering wheel or maybe even a bed?
- Will we still need parking attendants and carparks?
- Do we own the car or can we build a greenery where the carport is placed today?
- Is car cleaning going to be an investment field?
- Will cab drivers become redundant or will we see a new market for car butlers?

Practice asking questions and remember it's not a game about being the smartest kids in class or being right. It's all about looking for new opportunities.

Your Brain Can Predict the Future

One of the biggest discoveries in the field of Neuroscience is the fact that our brain can predict the future. Every hour, every minute, every second, your brain is trying to guess what will happen next. Take a break and notice how many unconscious thoughts you have: What's for dinner? We need to pick up the kids from day care, pack our bags for the holiday, work we need to do. All these thoughts are making a noise.

Scientists call it 'the predictive mind.' Your neurons are constantly active and stimulate each other to test hypotheses based on sensory input from the surroundings. And it's all working to help you make the best decisions.

If your brain wasn't predictive, you wouldn't be able to play basketball. Or hockey. Or any kind of sport for that matter, where you must anticipate the ball's curve or track the runner's path. Right now, as you are reading this, your brain is calculating millions of little predictions, and the interesting and most important thing for you to know is that it does so based on the experiences you had in the past.

Whisper that to yourself: "My brain is predicting my future based on experiences in my past." It doesn't take current events, trends or new opportunities into account. It only makes use of information about last night or yesterday and what it knows you're already good at.

This explains a lot, for if we made reasonable decisions based on what happens in our environment, we would only buy clothes we can actually fit, we wouldn't stay in dysfunctional relationships and we would definitely quit our jobs, if we felt it was pointless and without meaning.

But we don't think of the future as a space for decision-making. We use the past, our feelings, other people's needs, old traumas, worries, wishful thinking, hope and group pressure instead.

If you were driving a car, it would be the same if you used the rearview mirror instead of looking out of the windshield, while all the passengers were disturbing you with traffic warnings and well-meaning comments about the things that can go wrong.

If you've been fast and focused all your life and primarily followed the other cars on the highway of life, you'll easily forget about the small detours and the thousands of opportunities to do something different. Forward or backward are your only options and being stuck is the worst that can happen.

But you do have options and they are already there even though you can't see them. We lose what we don't practice, so if you don't practice altering the course of our life, it will feel increasingly difficult and impossible for you to actually do it. You'll be afraid of losing, because you don't know what you'll get.

So here's the point: If you don't practice taking a right turn every once in a while and drive somewhere else, you become a back-seat passenger in your own life. And what do they typically do? Paper work, computer games, watch a movie, eat, sleep, complaining.

This is a standby mode that you can continue living in for the rest of your life. Comfort over freedom. A life in which all types of disturbance are annoying, unless they evolve around eating or peeing. From your position in the back seat you've handed over the control of the vehicle to the driver, and then one day there's another driver, who wants other passengers on board, meaning you're out on your ass because you didn't invest in acquiring new skills or building a network.

Seen from the tribal perspective, it's a disaster to lose the ride, but from a Planetary point of view, it's a gift from above delivered in the rain by a deserted highway exit. We're all fired eventually anyway, and then the MBS wakes up. What should we do now? What is new and exciting? And then you become scared as hell, and thank you very much for that! For you can't be courageous if you're not also a little scared.

So, move over and take the front seat and set the course for the
Planetary future and get ready for magic. Your predictive brain is
ready. The part of you that just loves an adventure is excited and
dancing like a kid before ice cream.

What To Do?

Start every day by doing something that makes you happy and gives
you energy. Ban all brainwaves that sing a sour song and never show
up in the game (or at work) with a sour face and dragging wrists.

The first couple of hours, you don't have to be a fountain of energy
sprinkling jokes all over. It's perfectly okay to just be. Maybe it's
enough to stay in bed a little longer and stretch like a kitty cat. Maybe
it's enough to leave 15 minutes earlier, so you have time to actually talk
to your kids on the way to school. Or what about eating a chocolate
croissant veery slowly? Or dancing and singing in the shower, or
writing a few pages on your future bestseller?

Your past is only controlling you because you're repeating its stories.
Break the habit by introducing small time pockets of magic and
happiness. Make up new stories. Indulge in daydreaming about your
life the same way you would plan your next vacation. Tell yourself that
your past defines you just as much as the wake defines the course of a
boat.

Your Brain Has Incredible Memory and Processing Power

Your brain can analyze the past and predict the future because it is
more impressive than the most impressive super computer. A recent
guess is that the brain's capacity is as big as 2,5 petabyte, which is the
same as all the accumulated technology we've created so far, when
everything is connected in the global, digital and analogue network
called 'the Internet of Things.' Talk about mind-blowing!

The recognition of the magic potential of our brain evolved in tandem with the development of artificial intelligence, digitization, smart data and machine learning. No doubts that technology can store a lot of data, process it and produce clever solutions, but our own brain has super powers of its own and in such a scale, too, that it actually outruns all other machines known to man.

The challenge, though, is that we don't have a whole lot of RAM or short-term memory.

Your brain's short-term memory can only hold a limited amount of information in a relatively short period of time. So even if your brain has petabyte potential, it will easily be distracted by input of as little as 10-20 megabyte. On the one hand, this enables you to focus. One the other, you're likely to waste your time on insignificant things like a picture of a cute puppy, gazing queues on the highway or clickbait content in the tabloids. Similarly, the latest business buzzwords like 'robustness' or 'disruption' can hijack the board and management agendas for months!

Your tribal brain is easily distracted when you're hungry, scared or tired. If you kickstart your day with social media browsing, even if it's just for 5-10 minutes, or spend time stressing over your to-do list, the amount of unconscious decisions about anything from food to what to wear, dull meetings… well, you will have used up all the processing power for the day before you even get dressed. And, when you get back home after work, you'll get comfy on the couch and continue the routine with zero energy left to create and work on your future. Your potential is humongous, but your ability to put it to good use is only limited. So, if you have a feeling that there's something good inside of you, but you don't have a clue as to how to get it out, then join the club! 80% of all adults most likely feel the same. A report from the now-defunct SFI (The Danish National Research Center for Welfare) confirmed this. Unfortunately, the majority of adults didn't believe that it was their own responsibility to release this potential. It was either up to their boss or society.

In the future, nobody will come and rescue you. There will be no tribal hero like Bruce Willis saving you from the burning building. And there certainly won't be a union steward or headhunter telling you, "Excuse me, you seem to be waisting your potential, let's fix it and place you on the right shelf."

For better or worse, we're all doomed to freedom, to finding our own way, beliefs and way of life. On the road to our vantage point we can pluck and taste everything the world has to offer. The good life is not 'a la carte,' it's a buffet you share with the rest of humanity. And only you can decide how it tastes and if you like it. Only you know how the future feels, how to experience and appreciate a magic moment. We'd love to help you out, but some things you can only do yourself.

As futurists, we imagine that the full blown Planetary mode will make it possible for us to integrate on a much bigger scale than we do today. We're already using words like 'intuition' and 'sensitivity' and talk about 'good or bad energy,' and say things like, "What a great atmosphere in this room." We are sensing not just ourselves, but our fellow human beings as well.

Like we said, this hidden superpower might be the reason why so many people today are struggling with stress, restlessness, depression, mental issues, anxiety, ADHD, etc. The brain (especially in children and young people) is evolving to accommodate hyper complexity. Which makes sense, because why should we try to figure it out on our own, if the world is hyper complex and connected? Our super brain is searching for interconnectedness in empathetic and safe, but also destructive and constructive-creative communities. With this interconnectedness follows a series of emotions and discomfort that you mistake for your own. But in reality it belongs to everyone else. No wonder that we're so angry and tired, feeling lonely and develop apathy, because we constantly have to digest, address and respond to so many different things and input.

What To Do?

Relax! Visions are not to be forced, so take a break when you get a
headache or become frustrated. If you sense emotions or an unrest
that you don't understand, ask yourself if it's your own emotions and
unrest? The last thing you need is being a co-dependent junkie preying
on someone else's feelings. Let go of the thoughts and problems
and let your unconscious brain take over. Everything that happens,
happens outside the RAM, when you are daydreaming, get bored,
spend time in nature and listen to the world, collect new impressions
and when you let the pieces fall into place wherever they like. This is
where the shit gets real.

The visionary work where you speak, set up goals and present your
trends and ideas to others and collect feedback is important. But it is
just as important to let the brain rest and give it some quiet time. Let it
work for you.

Your Brain's Autopilot

Because your brain has to process millions of input every day, it has its
own autopilot, which it can turn on and off as it likes. You're already
familiar with it, its made up of your habits, routines and the behavior
that all sit on your backbone. One moment you can be outside
riding your bike and in the next, you're making a lasagne without
consciously referring to the recipe and making a feast. The autopilot
has automated a ridiculously big amount of important information
that will set you free to focus on other things. This is why you can
remember your first phone number, can ride a bike even though you
don't rehearse the skill or know the lyrics to a children's song you
haven't sung in 20 years.

Physically, the autopilot is placed in the so-called 'default mode
network'. It's a part of the brain that stores the procedural memory.
A procedure (or rules) that you can learn and which works for you
constitutes a body of knowledge that can be automated. It will become

your 'default setting,' and because your brain is constantly predicting the world around you, a well-established default mode network will give you an evolutionary advantage.

Your autopilot also processes your tacit knowledge, meaning all the things you know how to do without being able to explain it. Swimming, speaking in front of large groups of people, identifying the important issues in financial statements, being an experienced craftsman, calming babies down, singing, dancing, etc.

If your autopilot is well functioning and you remember to update it, you'll be an incredibly attractive person. You will land the good jobs, get a high salary, you'll be loved by your family and friends. Because you've got your shit in order. Without being able to explain and even without spending a lot of energy.

One of the important reasons why people in the future will get so generously paid is that they have capabilities that can't be replaced by a robot or another person. When who you are and what you can do is combined with your personality and your ability to continuously updating your brain's autopilot, you become invaluable. If on top of this you are also a nice and likeable person, what a catch you'll be!

There are two ways to update your autopilot. And what's really awesome is that it turns out that your autopilot is actively learning when you're preoccupied with brain activities related to a higher order such as re-imagining the future, looking at the world from the perspective of others and solving creative problems.

But what could prove a potential bomb under your prospect, as the mother of modern nursing, the British nurse, Florence Nightingale, said, "Little can be done under the spirit of fear." And how right she was, for when you're scared, worried or stressed out, evolution comes at an immediate halt.

You can't build a future on fear! In order to update your brain with new and important knowledge, you need to set yourself free by emptying your head and make room for an empty space free of thoughts, old stories and bad habits. Just spend 1-5 minutes per day doing nothing. The nothingness will develop your autopilot in a good way as your default mode network thrives when you're creating another reality for the brain by relaxing, daydreaming and letting your thoughts run loose.

Science has adapted this idea of creating an alternative reality. In the treatment of brain damages, traumas and brain diseases, things like holograms, Virtual Reality and psychopharmaceuticals like LSD, ayahuasca and mushrooms are gaining ground. These methods are tricking the brain into thinking that there's another world, another reality. The brain then gets an opportunity to learn new procedures, which means that the autopilot is re-programmed faster and under more safe circumstances. Just like pilots learning to fly or doctors practicing on virtual 3D-models – or teenagers playing PlayStation.

In our network of futurists, most people agree that the mechanisms that we're using to update disabilities (sight, hearing, memory, prosthesis, etc.) will also at one point be used with ordinary people even though we're well and healthy. Similarly, computer games with their thrilling and captivating universes will become a place we visit to re-program, practice and upgrade our software, if you like. It will be widely accepted to have this opportunity to practice washing older people, revive people who has suffered from a heart attack or grow potatoes on Mars.

What To Do?

The autopilot is your best card when you're hunting for the planetary future. You just need to reprogram it from past to future, from collecting ballast in the patterns of yore to making decisions based on visualizations about the future, like for instance the things you need to master tomorrow instead of yesterday.

When you were a small child, the autopilot helped you learn all your firsts – eating, crawling, walking, speaking, brushing your teeth. The common denominator is that somebody once believed that you could do it, that you had the necessary perseverance and that you could learn the right techniques. You developed your own method and didn't quit when you fell off the bicycle and because your parents didn't lose faith even though it took you longer to learn how to walk.

Your bad habits can be changed, but you need to make an active decision to do it and then practice, practice, practice your new good habits, which you'll need in the future you predict.

When you want to change a habit, a rule of thumb is to think about it as 'a hundred days of coercive action.' On average, it takes about 21 days to create a new habit, but your brain needs time to reboot, because the process of rewiring the connections between the nerve cells takes time.

The most important thing is your will to be a visionary and you ability to hold on to that decision, also when at first you really suck at it.

In the Now, the Die Is Cast – The Decisions Have Been Made

In the light of what we just described, that your brain has an autopilot and predicts the future on the basis of past experiences, what we're about to say might not come as a surprise. Still, one of the most spooky things in recent brain research is the discovery that the brain decides long before you decide. Crazy, right? Scientists have been able to measure how the decisions of test subjects are unconsciously made up to 10 seconds before they become aware of it.

The ultimate question, then, is if we have a free will at all? Are we the protagonist in our own movie or are we merely extras on set? Are we nothing but products of the choices we made in the past?

This recognition is the key to ultimate freedom and it provides three important points bear in mind:

- In the now, the die is cast.
- The decision you make in the now is the result of all decisions you've made previously.
- When you consciously know this, you can program your autopilot to make decisions based on the future rather than the past.

Discovering that the brain prevents you from making enlightened, conscious choices is scary. But then again, it's probably the best absolution you'll come across. Think about the freedom it brings and how much energy you can relocate from the eternal battle against yourself to visualizations about making better choices going forward.

Winston Churchill, the former British Prime Minister, had the upper hand when he noted that the easiest way to become the person you want to be is to imagine that you already are that person and then acting accordingly.

The fact that the die is cast in the now explains why it's so difficult to break free of old habits and change our behavior. When time and time again you're giving yourself a hard time and you're feeling guilty that you don't work out enough or eat too many sweets and blame yourself for yelling at the kids too much, remember it's not your fault. It's not the fault of the present-you.

The blame is on the past-you, on your traumas, old demons and all the decisions you previously made that weren't really yours. And what good comes out of blame anyway? Forgive yourself and sprinkle some sweet love and compassion – give yourself a hug!

Because the die is cast in the now, the present-you has an important job of visualizing future magic and letting go of the old bullshit.

WHAT TO DO?

Stop yourself in the now.

Say, "Well, well" and be conscious about the reasons why you make this particular decision, what principles or habits make it feel spontaneous, right or necessary? Just take five (or ten) and you'll break the spell of the autopilot. If you're able to make a better decision, congratulations! If not, then no worries! It's extremely difficult to change the now, but the force of the future is with you!

Cultivate visualization and follow the magic.

When you allow your brain the daily practice of processing new knowledge by saying, "Well, well," playing and experimenting, making mistakes and setting yourself free, you're actually activating the enormous processing powers of your brain.

Have a look at the future-you: What would the imaginary best version of you do in this situation tomorrow? Play out the different scenarios using colors, sounds and emotions. Watch who you become and then be this person, act the part. Notice how it feels and see what this version of you sees, feels and believes. What magic moments in your future are worth fighting for? Daydream a little more every day, five minutes will do just fine.

Make your own decisions.

Decisions make you bloom and grow. Imagine that your decisions are already out there and that they come from your vantage point and it's your job to be able to recognize them.

If you make all your decisions based on what other people expect, their mindset and obligations, etc., you'll mess up your life and in time lose the unique strength of your vantage point.

You Produce New Brain Cells Every Day

For thousands of years, the main thesis in brain research was that the neurogenesis of the brain (the formation of new brain cells) either stopped immediately after we are born or in the early childhood. From then on, it was down hill until at the end of life, a human being would only have a few sad brain cells left.

Science no longer believes this.

One of the most controversial discoveries in the history of brain research was when scientists in the 1960s discovered that the brain is reproducing new brain cells every day. However, it seems like we're only allowed to keep them, if we make new use of them.

The results are not unanimous though. First of all, scientists disagree about the very location of neurogenesis within the brain and what that means. Some believe that traumas in the brain are irreversible, while others believe that the brain is extremely plastic and designed by our thoughts and actions, that it knows how to self-repair, self-heal throughout our whole lives.

The German physicist Albert Einstein (1879-1955) said that there are two ways to live:

As if nothing is a miracle, or as if everything is a miracle.

At this point, we recommend the miracle, since neurogenesis is a desired scenario. If we assume that we're producing new brain cells every day throughout life, but that we have to learn new things and do something different and out of the ordinary in order to keep them, it will mean a great deal for the way we live, work, feel and settle in our lives. We would shy away from routine work and make an effort to learn and try new things. Neurogenesis means that brain damages can be restored and that old age will be something completely different that what our tribal past dictates. It has potential to be the planetary phase of life where we're wiser and more innovative than ever before.

There are many indications, however, that it will only happen if you truly believe and cultivate it by learning new things and make a habit of breaking habits.

What To Do?

Life isn't over just because you age and get older. The concept of old age didn't exist before we invented retirement. And maybe old is something you become, when you feel old, not when everybody else start to treat you like a feeble fogey. So don't grow old the uncool way.

Choose curiosity instead and decide to learn new things throughout life because you need it and just … because. It's what we call 'learning just in time and just because.'

Cultivate your life like a garden. Don't exhaust the soil by growing the same crops over and over again. Let it lie fallow and change the seed to let new and exciting things happen in your life. You are able to learn and improve no matter how old you are. You can change your social circle, you can travel, change character, personality, your career, interests, you can even become a futurist … for, no matter what you believe, you will be right.

Your Brain Thinks In Patterns and Stories

Every second, the brain processes huge amounts of information, it sorts the not important and presents the important information. The brain can execute this routine in a split second because it is really good at recognizing patterns.

Your inner life consists of movies and pictures, patterns and integral wholes, not single detached unities. When something is not coherent, you're unconsciously using brain capacity on fixing the potholes in the pictures. And because the brain works in this way, you'll never see reality as it really is. You'll see reality as you are. Unless you're a small child, the brain compares all new input to what's already known.

Through patterns of experience we can build a bridge to one another. If you tell me your stomach hurts, I'll ask myself what pain to the stomach feels like to me, "Is it an exam-like pain or did you eat something that doesn't agree with you?"

Patterns of experience are just an expression of story. In recognizing patterns, our brain doesn't like things that are not coherent.

And this is why we ponder, create meaning and fill in the gaps to make it fit the reality we want to create. When an idol like Elvis Presley (1935-1977) died, a lot of people couldn't handle creating a new story, so they came up with a more digestible narrative, a conspiracy theory proposing that he had just retired and was still alive somewhere out there. And then all of a sudden they had something in common with people who also had a hard time accepting that he actually died.

Since the beginning of time, stories and storytelling have been the glue that connected people and tied them together. Telling tall tales around the camp fire, ghost stories about witches and trolls, religions and political ideologies, books and movies. Stories provide meaning and create a calm within us, but they also push our motivation for changing things.

The brain is hardwired for creating, remembering and reproducing stories. Another theory states that there are 'memes' (cultural genes of sorts) that can occupy our brain and encourage us to share them with others. Memes are urban legends, jokes, obsessive thoughts, myths, gossip and fake news. When you can't get a song out of your head, or you're obsessed with an idea that just won't go away. Supporters of the meme theory will say that it's not your fault, but that it's the memes reproducing themselves by having you telling the stories again and again. That a story is in fact a product of the imagination or alternative facts without a foundation doesn't have to impact your desire to share a story with others. Our need to be a part of a shared story is often more important than recognizing the cold facts of reality. Even scientists agree it's difficult to give up on a great theory just because it isn't consistent with reality.

So many institutions and organizations today are in a tight spot regarding their stories. Take a look at the trade union movement, journalism, religion, political ideologies, the nation state and family. Every time we say, "We usually …" Or, "We need to respect the past…" Or when we try to match our opinions up against those who think and believe the same as we do in so-called 'filter bubbles', we're basically more interested in preserving the story and the patterns that make us feel safe. Leaving a story behind is like letting yourself and the others down.

Other stories thrive: in movies, books, autobiographies, podcasts, sports, science fiction, computer games. And on the negative side: terrorism, extremism, populism and criminal organizations. And then the trend we call 'My story,' where the individual is piecing together his or her own reality instead of reflecting and comparing it to everyone else's.

A young man once came up to us and said, "I'm interested in my own future, in my own story, because history is HIS story, you know, somebody else's story." To the older generations, this comes across as self-absorbed. To the younger generations, on the other hand, it's a natural consequence of having no story to unite them in a meaningful way. Besides the monarchy, popular TV-shows and soccer games, that is. We are on the verge of a future, where superpowers are still fighting each other to defend the old stories about who they used to be, while brands, creative marketing, social media and a lot of other rascals are fighting to get your brain's attention. On the one hand, we will see more closed story circles, where we have to buy the entire message to take part. On the other hand, open stories or movements, in which you create the story based on your personal needs, will also see the light of day.

Does it sound chaotic? Well, you're right. One thing is certain, though: We will see more noise and fights over who's telling the best story.

What To Do?

Remind yourself every day that what you know about reality is not, in fact, reality. It's your story about reality.

This means that if you come across something exciting that didn't exist before, you brain will not understand it immediately. This is why you need to keep an open mind toward the things you can't predict with the knowledge you have today. You need to be able to wonder, because when you're wondering, you'll look at what's new without categorizing and labelling it. It'll just be "Wow!"

The spiritual teacher and best-selling author, Eckhardt Tolle, became famous when he published the book 'The Power of Now' about the importance of being in the now. Let's add to this the power of 'staying in the know' where you're aware of the situation and accept that it's okay to be all at sea and not understanding a damn thing. Yet. When you stay in the know, you're on top of it and have faith that you'll land on your two feet again. For, the fact is that we learn new stuff 'in relation to' and that stories can be so powerful that they hijack our thinking processes. Being curious is an important strategy. And being able to seek out irritation and wanting to talk to people who are different from you and putting yourself in the shoes of others will be important qualities. So, dig deep into the well of knowledge, introduce a little poetry in your life and train your muscle of empathy.

The concept of empathy comes from the arts where it refers to the viewer being able to feel what the artist across time and space wants you to feel. Without using any words, empathy makes us able to travel into the minds, bodies and souls of other people and the stories of previous times. Empathy is crucial if we want to succeed and win the future.

Interesting stories are abundant. Don't just stick to one. Help create new stories and don't be afraid of things that are annoying or things we haven't seen before.

As a futurist, you know that our brains are masters of recognizing patterns. In the borderland between Tribal and Planetary, you need to be able to break with the well-known and look at the new, while the patterns are still unclear to you. And remember to ask questions and wonder! The world will not be wonderful, before you know the gift of wonder.

Your Brain Perceives the Future as Projected Memories

Your brain uses stories to predict the future. When you think you're thinking about the future, you're actually just creating a projected memory. Here's an example: If you hear the word 'vacation,' your brain will go over all the slides in your mental archive until it finds one that says 'vacation.' This slide will then be projected, often also enhanced, so you can improve it. Your grandparents would not be able to imagine 'vacation' as a trip to Thailand that includes 12 water chutes and a visit to an animal friendly nursing home for elephants. For them, 'vacation' meant going for a ride to the sea side. In your parents' time, the world became a little bigger and so their vision of a 'vacation' could be a bus trip to the Garda Lake. As we speak (in 2020), you run the risk of being called a 'climate bully' if you post images on Instagram from your vacation somewhere far away. So, to the next and future generations, maybe lying in a bathtub at home wearing Virtual Reality goggles will be the common vision of a 'vacation'.

Your idea of a 'vacation' depends on your prospect and your vantage point, on who you are, the opportunities you see and who you want to be in the world. Not to mention the ways in which you use your brain. If you don't feed your brain with new and exciting trends, it won't be able to predict the future.

Just looking at photos from other people's vacation will lure the brain into making new and interesting projected memories. Memories about the future. And because we love to tell stories, in time, these projected memories will be richer and full of details that might not reflect the reality as it was. And this goes for the good things as well as the ones, which are a tad more scary, dramatic and frightening.

Projected memories provide a powerful tool to win the future. Everything used to be new and dangerous, so just believing that you've tried something before or heard about other people's experiences will give you a sense of comfort. Maybe we don't dream about traveling the world and imagine what's going to happen. And this is why we love to hear and see photos of people who sailed around the world with their family. When someone embarked on a journey, we borrow their stories and make them our own.

Things will start to crash, however, when we don't have positive memories to project. Like in the spring of 2020, when people ran out to hoard toilet paper and canned foods, because they got scared of the general lock-down due to the rapid spread of the Corona-virus (Covid-19) – a global pandemic the like of which no one had ever seen or experienced before. The trend 'the long life' is another great example of how people have lived long lives since the beginning of time, but we never quite knew what to do with the elderly. If you didn't have a family to take care of you, you would have to work until you died. Or, you would jump into the ocean and disappear in the waves or take a long walk into the woods never to be seen again. The penitentiary and the poorhouse were not exactly places of comfort, and our guess is that you're not super excited about the prospect of ending up somewhere like this when you get old, right? So when we contemplate the ageing society, the brain is not choosing a projected memory of a dynamic, wise and creative Indian chief working rebelliously to spread joy in the community. It will choose an image of shrunken and sour prunes, project it and make it look a lot worse. And all of a sudden, the future is full of old people we don't really know where to place and whom we are a bit scared of.

Well, well.

What To Do?

Ask yourself where you're already rehearsing your vision and creative powers? Maybe it's in sports, cooking, travel & events, or maybe you are superb at making up fun activities? When do you feel at home as a visionary?

Expand this belief to your life in general. If you can in one area, there's no reason why you shouldn't be able too in others? With a little research, study trips and by collecting lots and lots of trends, cases and experiences, you can build your future on new projected memories.

A projected memory is like a movie we want to star in. So get out and do or create something. The future is not made in meeting rooms displaying PowerPoint presentations. You need to go out and play Indiana Jones or Lara Croft and make the every day life your vacation, the place you love to be. And you need to play as there is an indication that exercising makes your body believe in you. And the more positive memories about your own accomplishments you can make, the more the brain will have in store. So follow your kids up into that tree, explore the secrets paths in the forrest and dive deep into the bottom of the fiord.

There's also increasing evidence that the bacterial flora in your digestion impacts on your ability to imagine the future as well as your mood and your thoughts. So eat some cabbage, abstain from food every now and then and treat your intestinal bacteria nicely.

You Forget That You Forgot

In order to save energy and clear out the system, your three brains are house cleaning while you sleep. The good news is that you feel rested and refreshed, ready to begin the day, when you wake up. The bad news is that you forget a lot of stuff, too. You might even forget that you forgot. Great ideas, visions, New Year resolutions and dreams go down the drain as long as they remain faint and vague ideas about the future that are not backed by habits and rules in your procedural network.

What To Do?

You need to program yourself to kickstart your vision as soon as you wake up. Bruce Lee famously had his vision written down in a letter on his nightstand which he would read out loud every morning before getting out of bed. Einstein used to go to bed asking a question to which he woke up with an answer to the next day, for as he reflected, "It's not that I am so smart, I just stay with my problems longer." Henrik has put up a big poster on his bedroom wall, which he looks at even before he looks at his beautiful wife in the morning.

You need to stir your visionary brain into action and feel the magnetism of your future magic moments with every brain and every cell.

You Remember the Wrong Things

As if that wasn't enough, besides forgetting, you also remember the wrong things. Damn! Some scientists think that 5-20% of what you think you can remember is actually false memories or recollections, meaning that these things never actually happened to you! They might have happened to someone in your family or to a friend of yours, or maybe you saw it in a movie. But either you told the story or let it unfold in your thoughts so often that eventually, your brain could no longer tell the difference between imagination and reality. You can be convinced that it was you who were once forgotten at the grocery store (and not you sister), or you can claim to have seen a UFO. The fact remains that it happened to someone else or that the memory crept in on you while you fell asleep at the cinema.

In short: You're a hot mess! You think your past is steady and secure and that the future is uncertain. The truth is that your past is just as abstract as your future. Adding to that, it's also full of holes and influenced by what you choose to remember. Except the UFO-part, though. UFOs are real!

What To Do?

Let go of all the things you don't want weighing you down, the things that are noisy and loud. Think of your three brains as a garden – what you cultivate will sprout. The seeds you don't want to grow, you'll have to weed out every now and then. And finally, you need to take care of your garden to make sure you can thrive in it. It has to make you happy and work for you.

In Planetary, you should think about others besides you and yours, for the fruits of whatever you create or clean up might not be harvested in your lifetime. Like the Chinese proverb goes, "The true meaning of life is to plant trees under whose shade you do not expect to sit."

Cheat Sheet: Wake Up Your MBS And Activate Your Future Sense

- Be curious and allow yourself to be surprised by new things. To wonder and say, "Well, well" or "Wow!" must be your knee-jerk reaction.
- Unconsciously, you are constantly predicting and testing hypotheses and scenarios. Practice presenting them and discussing different scenarios and dilemmas with others.
- You brain loves puzzle games and is constantly looking for patterns. Feed it with lots of pieces to play with in the form of trends.
- We easily forget and lose the thread when it comes to learning new things. Write down the things you want to remember and take pictures. Let the patterns find themselves.
- Learn what you need to learn about the future and then let it go again. Otherwise you end up repeating the past. Have your buddy help you reveal your patterns to yourself.
- The decision you make in the now is usually a product of decisions

you made in the past.

- The more you let the past decide, the less of the future is clear for you to see. If you're under a lot of pressure or are stressed out, it's difficult bordering on impossible to think and be visionary. So, create a new story about yourself that makes it easier for you to change what needs to be changed.
- When you're feeling comfortable, are daydreaming and are laying low, your autopilot is updating. So relax! Every day. Find some pockets of time to take a break and just be kind to yourself and the future.
- When you imagine the future and look at the world from the point of view of others or do something creative, your autopilot is also updating.
- Magic moments are the most important thing to bring from the past. Make an effort to experience and truly feel them when they occur. Which ones do you remember the best?
- In theory, it takes an average of 15 weeks of coercive action to design a new and magical brain, a full-blown MBS which is attuned to the future. Only then can you think the thoughts you want to think and decide for yourself which feelings you need to navigate with. Cultivate your visualization skills and creative powers every day to help your procedural memory update your autopilot.
- Enjoy the fact that everything is working for you. Your brain is your best friend, your heart loves you and your soul just want to play.

How to Control the Tribal Brain

Up until this point, we've proposed the idea that the future is open and you have a super potent and future-minded brain that can make a big difference for millions of people in a rather happy-go-lucky manner.

But what if the big bad wolf lies in wait around the corner? And yesterday, you stepped in dog poo? What guarantee do you have that you won't be stepping in dog shit again and again? And what if

everything goes wrong and nobody likes you? Or even worse, what
if everything becomes a big success and still nobody likes you? Fuck,
fuck, fuck! Better stay home then and do what you usually do. After
all, you do know what that is.

Your planetary brain is your best friend, but the tribal brain hides in
the back whether you like it or not. And it's the tribal brain that makes
you bet safe. The tribal brain led you to where you are now and it runs
on old and primitive programs that are not easily disposable. Your
operating system carries a design that doesn't always work for you.
Feelings and thoughts are taking control of your life's agenda, if you
don't step up and take responsibility.

As a futurist, you have been chosen to build the bridge between the old
and the new world, between Tribal and Planetary, and so you should
know how the tribal brain works. Because, when you do know, you're
also able to control yourself and convince others to follow you. Yes,
it's all about manipulation, temptation, motivation and inspiration –
according to your needs and necessities, of course.

More, Bigger, Faster, Taller

Biologists have a concept they call 'supernatural stimulus.' In short,
it means that a lot of animals, including human beings, are prone to
liking something if it is bigger and more dominant, longer or taller
than average.

For example, you can make a small bird hatch out an ostrich egg.
How cute is that!? And baboon bums that are more red and very
big are so much more delicious, apparently, than little baboon bums.
And what's up with a deer living in the forest growing huge antlers,
or the bird of paradise flashing long feathers, puff and pom poms to
the jungle crowd? In our world, we call this having a nice brand. In
nature, it signals S. E. X., since animals become excited when the good
gets extra. Also, or maybe even because of the gorgeous look, you
compromise with certainty: "You're so hot and handsome, you must

possess extraordinary strength and magical powers in order to survive with all this paraphernalia of feathers and colors."

With people, supernatural stimulus means we can't stop looking when there's been an accident and we think buffets of abundance are so delicious. Others can't seem to get enough of big boob and muscles. And why is it that kids just love the big box the present was sent in?

Also. Take high-heeled shoes. They are kind of weird, aren't they? Originally, high-heeled shoes were used as riding shoes for soldiers, but later on, they took on with the nobility, who couldn't get them high enough. The taller you were, the more distinguished your ranking. One stilt shoe in particular lifted the wealthy men and women up to nearly 20 inches. Women, then, needed more fabric to make longer dresses, and men now relied on waiters to be able to walk. So much for keeping up appearances.

We are unconsciously attracted to more of what we already like whether or not it is good for us. We yearn for it, but does it makes us happy? Not always.

Acting on one's passion usually pays off. When we make an effort, joy often shows up on the other side of something we don't want to do. We don't always feel like talking a walk, but when we get back from an afternoon tour of the splendid exterior, we rarely look at each other and say, "We should never have done that." Also. Not many women are eager to give birth, but we are always really happy that we did have kids (despite the mixture of irritation and magic that comes with the job) that a lot of people choose to go through it over and over again.

The tribal brain finds it extremely difficult to navigate between desire and joy. According to the Google X boss, Mo Gawdat, it is one of the most important challenges of our time. Launching his planetary project 'A billion happy people,' he (and Google) works to share the message that we must cultivate what makes us happy and look out for what's fun. 'Happy' is an inner feeling of satisfaction in life, where you trust that everything will be alright and that your expectations as to what you can accomplish match the circumstances. 'Fun' is anything that entertains and makes you happy in the short run. Most people tend to pour more fun when in fact they're not happy. And that, says Mo, sucks.

Mo Gawdat's message is that our operating system needs an update. In a short while, the robots will be here and we are their parents. If they only watch us doing what we desire, they won't be able to make us happy. If we're only driven by desire, robots will grow up as kids in a dysfunctional family.

Mo's project is planetary in every respect. He doesn't define what makes you happy, he only states that it's your duty to figure it out and then share it with others, so that we can change the rules of the game together. Mo Gawdat wins his game when a billion people have found their happy place. What a view you'll get, Mo! For us futurists, the transition from Tribal to Planetary is very much about being able to sort impulses and taking a break whenever we feel a desire to explore if something will make us happy. The optimal future you could help create would be one that makes us happy and one that we desire – and vice versa. In this way, we'll only eat food for our own pleasure, and then society would be designed to actually support our choices and dilemmas.

And that's not how it works today…

Greed, Sex & Fear

When in your everyday life you face something new, there are certain things that your tribal brain wants you to respond to. It's already coded into your brain and it is the questions of:

1. Is it dangerous?
2. Can I eat it?
3. Can I fuck it?

Don't be ashamed, it's not your fault. Being seduced by sex, food, murder and being carried away by the latest fashion trend every now and then can feel like being taken by the undercurrent as if you didn't even have a choice.

For thousands of years, we've played in the Tribal mode, where survival depended on how well we adapted to the group. Nature was a place of danger, and so habits and routines concerning food and sex and all dangerous things were a way of securing one's survival.

If everybody had chased something new, humanity would never have created lifelong communities. We would never have acquired a common language, if people had only used words they just made up. We would have shared poisonous food with each other and killed off the entire herd. We would respect 'dangerous,' and without sex we wouldn't have reproduced – and by the way, sex was always a kind of currency, entertainment as well as a tool to solve conflicts.

We have our brain to thank for the fact that we actually survived in a dangerous world. If it hadn't kept a watch out for creatures that would kill us, or if it hadn't helped us find stuff to eat and produce some offspring, we wouldn't be where we are today.

If, on the other hand, the herd hadn't been willing to follow the few futurists, we would still be living in caves eating dead squirrels. Every human being has the capacity to dream, explore, chase, experiment and stand on the edge of despair with a tickling feeling. We love the security, but we also seek the rush of taking a leap of faith.

This is the dance your brain is self-practicing. On the one side, you've got the autopilot, your habits and your standard response, your desire to stay put in what feels safe and well-known (and where you can have popcorn while watching a horror movie).

On the other side, you find the future brain and the land of visions: the new and unknown, where risks are plenty and the opportunity to create something completely new and exciting reside.

The Tribal Brain Is 1/3 Hunter, 1/3 Collector, 1/3 Permanent Resident

In his book, 'Sapiens', the Israeli historian, Yuval Noah Harari, experiments with the hypothesis that establishing the agricultural society might have been the stupidest thing we ever did. Before that, we lived as hunter-collectors and we probably never led a more healthy, adventurous, self-supporting and functional life than at this point in time. Life was hard, yes, but we were equally robust and closely connected with nature and our communities. We kept a varied diet, exercised a lot and experienced something new every day. Life was dangerous, but so were we.

Obviously, it wasn't a life that spilled an awful lot for the weak and the sick, and it was normal to withdraw from the group, when you were no longer able to hunt or collect anymore. Retirement was not invented at that time, and if you became sick, isolation from the group was mandatory. Friends and family would put food out for you in the forest and if it wasn't picked up, it was a signal that you'd passed away and then the group would move on.

Fractions of the tribe were probably tired of constantly relocating, when they'd just sorted the camp and redecorated with beautifully painted rocks and bones. The need to settle and build something more permanent, cultivating the land, must have seemed attractive. Those who wanted to live the lives of nomads were free to do so.

The problem of the agricultural society, however, was the grain-based diet that rendered humanity less well-nourished. Work, food and life in general became a more one-sided affair. We had more children and they were more likely to survive. But the quality of life didn't improve accordingly. The time we used to spend on exploring the near surroundings was now spent on monotonous work, reparations and daily routines.

With boredom, the need for discipline, a set framework and systems that discouraged any entrepreneurial spirit and independence, arose.

Religion serves many purposes.

In the agricultural society, it was definitely to make people adjust and align, obey the not so physically strong and stand your ground while you waited for the payoff in the afterlife. We might not be hunters anymore, but we remained collectors.

When the nomad life was replaced with permanent residency, the rules of the game changed radically. For when you're not constantly relocating, you can save up money, own more stuff that you can carry and trade with one another. This in turn gave rise to the fear of losing, and so the need of being watched over and the urge to submit or take power over the other tribes prevailed. This new way of life made way for politics, struggles over power, borders, weapons and war as well as diplomacy, insurance and negotiations, in which everyone can have their share of the cake. Villages were transformed into cities that in time became nation states, in which the things we own and the area we come from define our identities and our place in society.

A lot of the things that tribal players are preoccupied with, especially politicians, deal with how equal, free and satisfied human beings can be within the framework of a system that takes for granted that its residents want to live, own, work and consume. Politics is basically distribution of resources and regulation of behavior. If you'd rather live your life as a knowledge nomad, a village idiot or don't want a PIN (Personal Identification Number), you're not really considered a co-player in the eyes of society. As a human being, you'd be free, but only in Tribal. If you place yourself outside the tribal framework, it doesn't take long before you're either diagnosed with something random or labeled a criminal.

This is not to say that Tribal is the same as Siberia or the purgatory. Throughout thousands of years, the Tribal mode gave great results. The challenge today, however, is that at this point in time, we're facing a series of global problems that can't be solved by players in possession of tribal brains and mindsets.

Amygdala Hijack

The fact that it's easy to get carried away is in professional terms called an 'amygdala hijack.' The amygdala is the name of a small area in the brain's temporal lope, which among other things is responsible for detecting fear and defence mechanisms, including post-traumatic stress. When the amygdala is hijacked, your thoughts run loose and you feel out of control. Your otherwise visionary and planetary thought process is being hijacked by your inner tribal caveman or -woman, and if you don't stop him/her, you'll live your life controlled by thoughts based on fear, sex and food.

Let the thoughts run loose for a little while and then simply stop! It's actually pretty simple. Whenever you feel your brain has run off due to another round of sex, greed and fear, then take a physical step back, breathe and say: "Well, well, aha, interesting." This will help you create a neutral space that allows to you to be you, think your own thoughts and control your own mood.

If you don't get in control, at best, you risk ending up in yet another situation where you see the future coming – you analyze and understand it, but you don't act on it. You don't have the time, nor the energy. Or else you lie low and wait for the future to go away, because it's way too complex to handle.

Luckily, there's hope.

Absorb the Tribal Brain into Your Planetary Brains

The fact is that your tribal brain only wants to protect you. It so desperately wants to be your best friend that oftentimes, it ends up as your worst enemy instead. You become what you're trying to escape. If you don't face your worst fear, your taboos and your weaknesses will come bite you in the ass in the end. So use your planetary consciousness to give your tribal brain a little TLC and listen to it the way you listen to all your thoughts and feelings.

You probably know a variation of the story about the Indian woman and the wolves. The woman's grandchildren asked her, if she would give them a piece of advice, for she had lived an extraordinary life. She said that inside of her, there had always lived a good wolf and a bad wolf, and that her mission in life was to keep the bad wolf away from the good wolf. To the question of who wins, she said: "The one I feed the most."

In the same way, you must learn how to feed (train) the good parts of your tribalistic, greedy, passionate, fearsome, merry and funny tribal brain. And whenever the evil part is snarling, you'll say with confidence, "I hear you, now go lie down, you're not getting anything from me!"

Basically, it's a decision you make if you want to think your own thoughts and use your emotions as a compass instead of letting them control you. Practice recognizing the habits and thought patterns that don't do you good and handle the ones you can't get rid of. Let it be as natural as breathing for you to meet and welcome the new and unknown with a "Well, well, aha, interesting" and end the war between your planetary brain of the future and your fearsome tribalistic brain that so desperately works to maintain the status quo.

Level 2
MEET THE
TABOO TROLL

FACE YOUR WORST FEAR

Chapter 5
Meet the taboo troll

Tribal and Planetary are connected by a bridge. Just like in the fairy tales, the bridge is guarded by a troll, the Taboo Troll. Tricks and weapons won't get you past this guy as he demands payment in the form of you facing your worst fear.

'Taboo' is an old Polynesian word that means 'forbidden magic' or 'the place we do not go.' Taboos are the things that we silently agree not to mention or talk about. It is the things we know don't work, but which we stubbornly hold on to, because the revelation or the new and unfamiliar feels uncomfortable and unsafe. Taboos usually serve as an advantage for those in power, be it in the family, in society, in the church, etc. And it absolutely drains those it affects. People in therapy are very often going because they struggle with someone close to them, who refuses to go to therapy. And the taboo is that they were exploited, sponged, drained or abused and have a hard time saying it out loud, because it would be 'hurtful to other people' or it provokes anxiety – for what if we say it out loud and things get worse? What if, in turn, we stopped being so evasive and instead worked to fix the potholes and put out the fire? Would everything explode? Our ancestors were hanged from their bowels for even suggesting that there are things we don't talk about.

In order to demystify the taboos, we usually refer to them as 'the evil cousin of the trend' as it sounds less nasty. Generally, we see no problem in talking about trends, whereas taboos are that part of the future we pretend doesn't exist. We know they are there, but they smell. Actually, taboos stink, and so they make us uncomfortable and frightened. Unconsciously, we sense a warning that the act of exposing the taboo will demolish our imagination and self-images. So instead, we make a fuss and avoid talking about it at all costs. In this way, taboos participate in the game of maintaining the old vantage points, which it's due time we let go.

Only when you face your taboos, look them in the eyes and talk about your fears, the things you'd hate talking about, you can seize the future. Until then, you will be doomed to repeat your mistakes and continue the loop of your past pattern again and again. You can see but not touch it. The future is just around the corner, yet so very distant and far away.

THE FUTURIST'S TOP 10: THINGS PEOPLE GENERALLY FEAR THE MOST

Nobody loves or misses me.
Nobody needs me.
Being kicked out of the community.
What I do doesn't make a difference.
Being successful.
Being perceived as 'over the top'.
Being perceived as 'to vague'.
Giving a speech or presenting something to others.
Being exposed or seen as a failure.
Waisting my own time or that of others.

THE FUTURIST'S TOP 10: THINGS PEOPLE GENERALLY WANT IN LIFE

Peace of mind.
Being loved for who I am by family and friends.
Well-being for others.
Being seen and heard with real interest (and receiving sincere and useful feedback).
Being part of a community that creates joy and success.
Being able to share my own success and surplus with others.
Sleeping well at night.
To evolve and learn throughout life.
Mastering something and experiencing that what I contribute to the world is meaningful.
To die with grace and dignity.

People living in a marriage in crisis can often see the elements of danger lurking in the horizon: They know a divorce is inevitable. Still, they don't act on it, because they become exhausted by the very thought of talking about the fact that they don't love each other like they once did. The taboo gets in the way and blocks the necessary conversation about loss, grief, and heartache. Not just the loss of physical and material things like the house, the car and heirlooms, but also the loss of love, intimacy and community. Living in a marital crisis means creating new images of self, it's no longer 'us' but only 'me and the kids… and maybe a new boyfriend or girlfriend.'

Often the taboos are hidden where life has become most comfortable.

Actually, comfort itself can be the taboo. There's nothing pleasant about admitting that the reason why you don't pursue your dreams is because you've become too friendly with the couch.

A few years ago, we worked for a large Scandinavian corporation. We talked about innovation, new work flows and scenarios. And then some more about innovation. And they were constantly setting up new meetings to evaluate and review the process with pie charts examining every detail. And we kept pushing them to go out and actually meet their customers, talking with them and taking a look at the real world and talk to colleagues in their field. But it was always canceled or postponed. Time and time again, we asked them to make decisions based on the trends they themselves had spotted, but then they just wanted to run another workshop on innovation, which of course was followed by another evaluation.

The underlying vision was always that they wanted to be the European Champion in customer service. They really liked all the trends and cases that involved ways to make customers of the future happy.

But there was one future they didn't like and we stumbled upon it by chance one day, when one of the good guys whispered in our ear that they were uncomfortable with answering the phone. "Well, then" we told them, "the European Championship is not really within reach, is it?"

Being afraid of answering the phone and actually talking with your customers might be connected to the fact that we moderns are afraid of offending or hurting other people. Or we worry that it'll be embarrassing because we feel unprepared. On the other side, we are being forced together everywhere we go these days. Architects, for instance, loves to make room for creativity hubs in their projects, and at home, they knock down all the walls so that the only room where there's actually room for privacy is the bathroom. Picture that! A 'conversational bathroom' – O Lord!

As human beings, we're just not cut out for spending a whole lot of time in big and open spaces. We need quiet and privacy and we need time dedicated to concentration and deep thinking. We also want to keep our privacy in the private sphere and also don't always answer the phone when it rings. But if you say that out loud, you're considered a reactionary grumbler, who's not open to change.

In the eternal hunt for creating communities where we can be together, in what the fancy term of 'innovative and creative relations' describes, the paradox remains that we've actually created more loneliness. We can be in the midst of a huge crowd, yet have a feeling of being lonely, because we're not seen or understood. From another perspective, we can quite easily stand being alone and without feeling lonely. Once this taboo is finally revealed, it will be exciting to explore 'togetherness' in the future.

Identifying taboos is a fun thing to do, because they are hidden in-between the lines of an open book. They will be whispered in your ear, when you ask.

And it's our experience that when they've finally been said out loud, people really love to talk about them. Only, the circumstances have to be right. It's like scratching a mosquito bite that's out of reach. A little shame and also really nice at the same time.

That is why is not surprising that taboos are easy to break down, when we finally find the courage to have go at it. A great tip is to let people write down their taboo(s) on small pieces of paper which are gathered in a hat and then read them out loud to the group. People are cracking with laughter when they hear that someone is afraid of being looked down upon, because she feels more wise, and another one is afraid of the very same thing, because he thinks he's more stupid that others. They now share a common fear, which has been deflated, and now have the freedom to move on without being afraid of being exposed.

The Taboo Troll is a blimp we ourselves inflate. The minute we face it and look it in the eye, all the things we previously considered dangerous and scary vanishes into thin air. And then we can move on.

Menstruation

The female cycle has never, as in N-E-V-E-R, been a topic
we like to talk about. It is the very incarnation of taboo.
Most men squirm at the thought of putting their girlfriend's
tampons and san pads on the counter at the store, and in the
ads, the blood is usually blue.

**BUT MENSTRUATION IS A DANGEROUS THING IN THE
WORLD!**

Look at the ways in which menstruation is described as
something that creeps in on women. BOOH! This is why the
ads are promising 'security,' 'safety,' and 'an opportunity
to live your life normally.' In brochures from the mid-
20th century, clinical and rational descriptions explain the
mechanisms of the female body without ever using words
like 'blood' and 'vagina.' Back in the olden days, women of
a certain standing would have a travel oven to burn the used
cloths. Out of sight, out of mind. If women did not have
access to various plastic aprons or mystic belts to use with
their undergarments, they would have to stay at home until
their period was over.

The tampon was patented in 1936 and with it Procter &
Gamble addressed a market that potentially included half
of the world's population. They presented a product that
no one had explicitly expressed a need for. Ever. It was
not that the need wasn't there or that there wasn't already
sanitation products available, it just hadn't been identified as
a commercial market. But just because the product doesn't
(yet) exist or the need hasn't been articulated, it doesn't
mean that we don't want it. The payoff by addressing the
taboo, in this case menstruation, was huge. In recent years,
the menstruation taboo is no longer a bloody affair (sorry,
we couldn't help ourselves), and ecology has also gained
some ground in this area. The blood is more red, but the
Taboo Troll continues to reign in places, where women are
still controlled by tribalistic and pseudo-religious myths and
patterns of fear.

Certain media bosses of higher ranking have told us that the arrogance they sometimes see in their profession (shouting debates and journalists emphasizing conflicts in society) is due to the fact that the journalists' training is of such a poor quality and not in keeping with the times. This makes it difficult to remain curious and so journalists become insecure. It invites a closed, professional circle, where bloggers are looked down upon as writers and where reading the newspaper is a civic duty.

From the tribal perspective, you'd be pissed off if someone accused you of not being good enough or competent enough. The Taboo Troll has the most magnificent ability to encourage us to recreate the very situation we fear the most. So when we don't face our fears and admit to ourselves that deep down we are afraid of becoming redundant, being kicked out or losing the things and the people that we love, we cannot invest in preventing it from happening. We become the spook in our own ghost story. We become the very thing we fear the most.

From a planetary perspective, on the other hand, you would immediately think that nobody is good or talented enough anymore. Hooray! Imagine if you had to be a lifelong learner acquiring the skills to master a lot of things. Wow! Again, curiosity is crucial for figuring out what we need to be good at and how we do so faster than before.

We do want to emphasize that rejecting a taboo is not a sign of evil or stupidity. The rejection is rather about the loss of power and the warm feeling of safety combined with the cold and uncomfortable feeling of not really knowing what to do and what to put instead. The taboo truly is a taboo-hoo. Psychology confirms this in emphasizing that an intervention that threatens our opportunity to show skill provokes a defensive or even aggressive attitude and releases negative emotions. Tn other words: Facing your taboos is an integral part of your hero's journey. It's the difference of being the superficial Prince Charming in 'Shrek' and the profound, but edgy King Aragorn in 'The Lord of the Rings.'

Always Accept Dangerous Knowledge About Potential Change

Where the trend holds important and meaningful information about potential changes, the taboo lets you know that something dangerous and challenging is on its way. It's something we need to know, but not necessarily have to act on right this minute.

We should be practicing ways in which we can deal with our taboos, but the question is how? It's perfectly normal to feel insecure and be cross and offended, but that doesn't mean that it's a strategically great move to bury your head in the sand, shoot the messenger or be mad with fury.

Instead you must activate your MBS and wake up your future sense.

You now know that the brain is categorizing and generating new thoughts on the basis of old knowledge and experience. When you choose to avoid the Taboo Troll, which means staying put in your pre-programmed conception of what the world looks like, you'll be mad and offended if somebody dares to mention the forbidden magic.

With an active MBS and future sense, you know to expect this reaction. You can predict it and then avoid taking it personally. Say instead, "Wow, that's interesting, look at me all cross and offended. Please, sweet buddy of mine, help me reveal my taboo and release my vision and creative powers."

What is it worth to you to be able to decode your behavioral patterns and then being able to identify the patterns of others? When you've had some time to digest it all and you see things from a new perspective, you'll be able to teach everybody else to look at the taboos with empathy and humor.

This is exactly what art, satire and stand-up comedians do. You can win popularity by consequently breaking with the taboos. A sense of occasion and timing is of course crucial. 'To soon?' the comedian asks if the joke attacking the taboo is still a little too nasty to swallow.

We can't be truly human together before we give each other the space
we need to address the taboos – when we let go of the childish need to
push away annoying people, to slander and talk dirty behind people's
backs and manipulate reality with the sole purpose of putting together
a team that will confirm that 'we are the best' and that the others are
idiots.

Only when we take responsibility for our own crap, heal our wounds
and traumas and say we're sorry, only then we'll realize that we're all,
in fact, amateurs. And then we can laugh about it.

When we're able to have a good time in spite of the things that annoy
us or seem scary, redemption immediately follows.

When you can begin to sense that magic and irritation are two sides
of the same coin, you've successfully crossed the bridge from Tribal to
Planetary.

Irritation and fear will have lost their power over you and can never
again hold you back.

And then the adventure truly begins.

Level 3
MAGIC AND
IRRITATION

NAVIGATE THE FUTURE

Chapter 6
Magic and irritation

There's a wonderful quote by the American poet, Mary Oliver (1935-2019), describing the magic moments of life.

"Ten times a day something happens to me like this – some strengthening throb of amazement – some good sweet empathic ping and swell. This is the first, the wildest and the wisest thing I know: that the soul exists and is built entirely out of attentiveness."

The magic moments are the little big things that give you a rush of joy, satisfaction, happiness or a sense of meaning. Magic moments are the point where things fall into place and your motivation and energy levels rise. Your soul is with you and all you need to do is to pay attention.

It's important to enjoy and experience these magic moments. When you feel the 'mmmh' of joy inside of you, then stop for a moment and take a physical or mental picture of the situation, write down what happened, or make a drawing to describe it. Don't overanalyze! When you have the magic moment in the palm of your hand, stop and say, "Oooh, wait a minute, wait a minute, I've got a magic moment here. Ahhh!"

Your pictures and notes are not additions to you never-ending to do-list. On the contrary, they are meant for your to be-list. You need magic moments in order to be able to connect the dots. Your magic moments will draw up a pattern leading you in the direction of the future you dream of deep down. Who wants to follow a vision with zero magic in it? Who longs for a future they can't feel and which is stripped of real and heartfelt joy? Your magic moments will help you figure out who you are in this world, what the world needs you to be and what trends you should navigate after.

A vision of the future that includes magic moments, in which your passion is on fire, will be far more motivating for you than yet another round of PowerPoint presentations.

Besides pointing you in the direction of the future you truly want, you can also use magic moments for other things.

Is your teenager not too keen on the future? Stop asking questions like, "What do want to be when you grow up?" Instead, you should create a mutual magic zone, where you dream about the future together and ask questions like, "Where do you really want to make a difference and who do you want to do it with?"

The future is brought to life when we can truly feel the magic – for you, your loved ones and your colleagues. If the talk is on vacations, our plans for the weekend, or something to do with sports, we get moving. Nobody wants to do stuff in their spare time that is boring bullshit. You need magic in your life. Every day. Preferably a lot. So from now on, begin to notice the things that ignite that feeling of magic. Within you.

You Run from Traumas and Hunt for Magic Moments

A trauma can reside in you for ever, while a magic moment evaporates as water on a heated hotplate. Maybe it's because we tend to cultivate our bad experiences and completely overlook the magic we already have in our lives.

Genetically, we're wired to chase the magic moments. Since the beginning of time, we've experienced these moments with food: When

we found berries in the forest and were full. In the community, by
sharing the food and watch the others' excitement. And, of course,
sex. If an orgasm lasted for three months, mankind had starved to
death a long time ago. This would explain why traumas affect us
deeply, while magic moments are brief and intense. If you dwell too
much on the good stuff, you'll lose the Yellow Jersey of evolution – at
least in the Tribal mode.

In the Planetary mode, magic moments are the sole and primary
reason we're here on Earth. So, when you're told, "You just have to act
your vibe," it really means that you should chase your magic moments.
By activating your MBS, you can use these moments to reprogram
your brain.

Now, hold on to your pantyhose! Magic moments are said to be
stored in the universe in what is called the cosmic web. Not only is the
brain and the cosmic web alike, there's also statistic evidence that the
uniformity is real! And so it's not only due to our ability to identify
patterns and belief that just because two things look alike, they are the
same.

The facts are these:

- Everything in the universe is made up of energy and relation.
- The brain is in principle the relation between brain cells shooting
  energy to one another.
- Borders are, scientifically speaking, an illusion and so there
  really doesn't exist a delimitation between ourselves and our
  surroundings. It's more like an atomic transition.
- Your magic moments (which is really a fancy way of saying,
  "Energy and relation, spot on") can impact on the surroundings –
  and the universe.

And this is why, time and time again, that you can experience an
alignment with the world. That you're attuned to the same wavelength
and feel the flow and know the feeling of being 'in sync.' Just like
a piano standing in the end of a room can make the strings in the

piano at the other end of the room vibrate when you play. Physically speaking, we're nothing, literally 'no thing,' as we're made up of energy in relation to another energy. Bad relations and bad energy is bad for your creative powers. With good energy and great relations, you can create whatever you want. You can create your very own magic! And upload it to the universe.

So, every time you experience a magic moment that you enjoy and roll in, you've reached the goal in the Planetary mode. If a modern vampire, narcissist or a nasty leech sucks and drain you, prepare for the power boosting energy that comes from getting rid of them and healing your wounds, so they can't come back. Your energy level is your energy level. Keep it high!

On your journey into the future, you need to surround yourself with people that build you up. You know, the types that exchange energy and who don't drain you. Imagine you're climbing a mountain. On the way up, you meet two spoiled tourists, who've lost their way and haven't prepared properly for the trip. You offer to take them along and share your food and tent with then. At the top, they take a lot of selfies, but conveniently leave you out of their pictures. Somehow, you end up saying yes to carrying all their luggage downhill, because 'it's good for your development.' And when you get down and back to the camp, they complain that the trip was cold and you brought tasteless food.

From this point, you're allowed to say, "Bye, bye," leave and walk past them. Go create your magic, even though it feels selfish. It's not! You're shaping your identity, not your ego. If you can't help it, it's because you have a 'despair trigger,' a trauma from the past that made a hole in you and which you try to refill by giving so much of yourself to others. The problem is that it doesn't work. What you seek in others, you need to be able to give yourself. This is pure and life-enhancing magic.

What Can You Do to Make Magic Win over Fear and Trauma?

Magic wins when you believe in it. Actually believing in yourself encourages you to practice, so that in the end, you know you can do it. The best place to begin is to experience the magic moments you already have. Grant yourself permission to enjoy them and have faith that the universe right there in that moment does the same.

By revisiting the magic moments of your life, by having lots of them and by sharing them with others, in time, you'll be good at imagining new magic moments. You'll make use of your brain's capability to recall memories from the past. Take pictures of situations that are magical to you and put them in a folder to make your own slide show to display as projected memories about the future. And make them colorful, rich and free.

Yes, we know. All this talk about magic and the universe can sound a little like gibberish mumbo jumbo. But what if magic is in fact the new normal and we're just not able to see it yet? Beliefs help shape the future and we have believed stuff in the past that was just as wacky as this.

Think about it for a moment: If it turns out that our theory holds water, that your magic moments are stored and saved in the universe, then a large part of the meaning of life must be that you should create your own magic – your energy in relation to others.

The meaning of life, in that case, will not be to be extremely productive and get busy doing a hole lot of stuff for others. The meaning is that you must discover and experience what magic moments are to you. And then share them with the world.

Go Look for Irritation

At its worst, the world is most annoying when it tries to tell you something you don't want to hear.

And people are most annoying when they are right.

The difference between a tourist and a futurist is to a large extent their willingness to look for irritation in order to become a stronger player. You'll lose your footing for a short while, but come back strengthened.

As the American journalist and feminist, Gloria Steinem, puts it:

** THE TRUTH WILL SET YOU FREE,
BUT FIRST, IT WILL PISS YOU OFF. **

By looking for irritation, you're mentally letting go of everything you previously thought to be true. You'll shake the bag of puzzle pieces and be ready to begin anew. You may compare it to training and exercising. When you're exercising you're irritating your muscles, because you know that the future-you will be stronger, even though it pains the present-you. In the same way, irritation tears old relations in your brain apart, so that you can piece them together again in new and more magical and planetary ways.

The more annoying it is, the greater the potential for magic.

Bad irritation

… is like a pebble in your shoe. It doesn't do you any good and you can't use it. Stop, take off the shoe and get rid of the pebble. Don't feel guilty, don't feel ashamed, you don't need it!

Good irritation

… hurts in the short run and builds you up in the long run. When we're physically exercising, we are actively destroying muscle fibers, which hurts like hell. But it will push and move you forward from entitlement to enlightenment.

You can't win the future if you keep hanging on to the past.

If you spot a trend you don't like, you will most likely be pissed off. Annoyed. Or else you'll put your head in the sand like an ostrich, or build a sand castle with those who share your beliefs. And then you can live there and observe the rise of the ocean levels.

It's what the typographers did in the 1980s, when the first wave of digitization hit. The cab drivers reacted in the same way in the 2010s, when the first services to rely on peer-to-peer economy were invented.

Have a lookout for the people who gets angry and closes their eyes when something new is on the way. For it might very well be your job to help them letting go of the old vantage point in order to conquer a new.

When you wear tribal glasses, it's perfectly natural to be upset and very, very, very angry – not to mention defensive – when a trend threatens to destroy the things you've been fighting for and built your identity on. Why can't we just stay put in what's comforting and safe? Why can't we just do like we always did? A reaction rooted in anger never did anybody any good.

If you see a future without magic, it's because your vantage point is old or simply wrong. It will create irritation and frustration, because your self-image falls out of step with reality. "If the rate of change on the outside exceeds the rate of change on the inside, the end is in sight," as the business man, Jack Welch, once said.

Case: From 'Ownership' to 'Access to' – What a Socialist Idea

When in 2005, we started talking about peer-to-peer economy (or the sharing economy), we were surprised to see how many hot-tempered reactions we got. In organizations within the Danish public sector, for instance, we were accused of promoting the disbandment of private property ownership. Especially in the municipalities and in media houses, C-level professionals got very hot-headed, and one guy actually came up to us and said, "This kind of socialist bullshit shouldn't be allowed to cross the border."

Socialism or not, peer-to-peer economy (P2P) is here to stay, for why own a summer cabin yourself, when you can have access to luxurious villas all over the world?

And why would you be collecting CD's with movies and music, when you can stream everything online? And why own your own car, when you can access and subscribe for self-driving cars in the near future? Imagine that the cars of the future are clean and nice, that you'll be able to sleep while moving from A to B, that you'll be entertained and are able to host meetings on the go. You won't be spending time and money on car parks, refueling or repairs. There will be a huge market for car cleaning and we will want to buy different plans for hosting meetings, breakfast, fun time with the kids, etc. And most likely, a dating service will launch a 'get laid'-app to present you with surprise passengers for your self-driving car ride. On that note: The car we all want will need a little cleaning… And a team of rebels will make sure that everything is run and financed by people's shares so that the profit is evenly distributed to as many citizens as possible instead of ending up in the pockets of yet another venture capital fund abroad.

The new platforms of the sharing economy speaks to the heart of a new type of consumer. For this is not about consuming. It's about having access to things we actually need. If I buy an expensive pram, I don't do it to brag or to boost my personal brand. I buy it for many reasons, one of which is that I'll be able to resell it and thus reducing the impact on the environment.

We will see the same transformation in the fashion industry. For, let's face it, most of us don't really need more clothes. No, girlfriend, we don't! We need better style. Yes, you too! We could get that, among other things, by sharing our closet with our friends instead of succumbing to the messy piles at home. The new P2P-platforms

challenge the nation state, the classic business community, the trade
unions, media houses and politicians to a degree we've never seen
before. And boy, are they annoyed! For what would they do if they no
longer 'owned' their customers, members, employees, markets and
citizens? The point is not that we must persuade or convince others of
the advantage by a certain trend. We need others to see the future as
it is, as it will be. The trends will come no matter what we do. Today,
when we meet old customers from 2005, they say, "Well, we thought
you two were a couple of nut cases, but it seems you were right after
all." Like we've won something. But that is not the point at all. We
only win if, in due time, we can make people see and recognize the
advantages of P2P. If we succeed, the best scenario for the sharing
economy will bee that a lot of people can care more about their
quality of life instead of a standard of life. In other words, we will
benefit from what we already have.

The alternative scenario that we all must own and consume like we
couldn't care less would take the resources of another 2, 3, 4, 5…
planets.

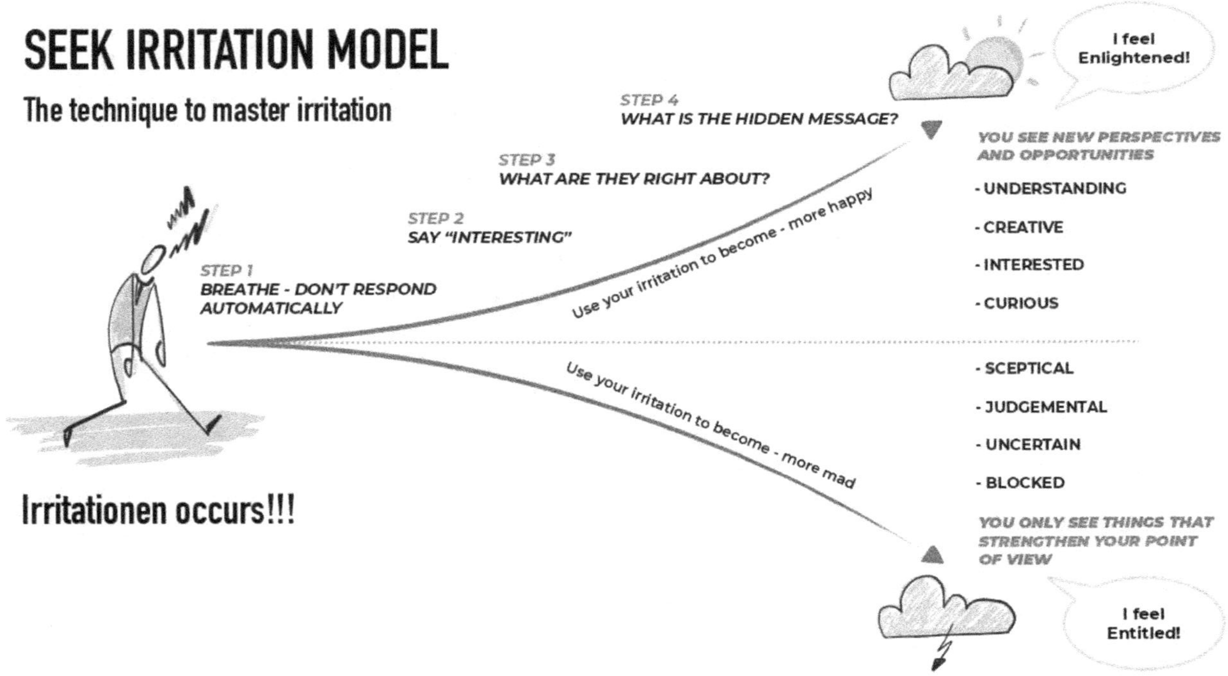
SEEK IRRITATION MODEL
The technique to master irritation
STEP 1
BREATHE - DON'T RESPOND AUTOMATICALLY
STEP 2
SAY "INTERESTING"
STEP 3
WHAT ARE THEY RIGHT ABOUT?
STEP 4
WHAT IS THE HIDDEN MESSAGE?
Use your irritation to become - more happy
Use your irritation to become - more mad
I feel Enlightened!
YOU SEE NEW PERSPECTIVES AND OPPORTUNITIES
- UNDERSTANDING
- CREATIVE
- INTERESTED
- CURIOUS
- SCEPTICAL
- JUDGEMENTAL
- UNCERTAIN
- BLOCKED
YOU ONLY SEE THINGS THAT STRENGTHEN YOUR POINT OF VIEW
I feel Entitled!
Irritationen occurs!!!

Irritation Is Your Personal Future Trainer

Irritation feels like a smoke bomb. You'll want to roll your eyes, take deeps sighs and find someone that will agree with you that people are gigantic assholes.

If your head is filled with smoke, you can't think clearly, and if you're playing in the Tribal mode, you'll fall into one of your autopilot's two reaction patterns, head first:

- You turn inward and become obsessed with your own thoughts and arguments. In order to feel safe, you seek the company of those who'll confirm your theses.

Or

- You turn the irritation outward and shoot the messenger, bang, bang! And then you make up a great story that justifies your deed, that you demand your rights or that you were offended!

If, on the other hand, you're playing in the Planetary mode, your line of thoughts will be quite different. You'll use your future sense to activate your curiosity, and you'll say, "Well, well, aha, interesting." You'll ask what the world is trying to say that you don't want to hear. It's alright if you yelled a little at first, "Aaaaaaaaargh, kill, destroy kill, kill!" We're pioneers and it is okay to fall into the pits. Have some Bearnaise sauce, bitch talk a little to your buddy, take a deep breath and then come back into the light.

By looking for irritation, you'll invite new perspectives to come to you and you'll look at the world without bias and presumptions. Irritation will hit you no matter what you do, so you might as well prepare for it. As a futurist, you're not waiting for irritation to show up at your doorstep. You go look for it, while you curiously waddle around in the taboos, the habits and your tribal mindset with a little political correctness on top.

If you're in Planetary, however, the Game of the Future rewards you for taking responsibility for your own shit. What part of a problem was your fault? What can you take responsibility for?

When you take responsibility, the dominos stop falling. Only players in Tribal will think it's fair to push all the problems in front of you, to others or to the future-you.

Let Go & Throw It Away

When you let go of your past, an old identity and last year's vantage point, you'll earn street credit. Nokia, for instance, was in the eyes of the general public totally bad ass for reinventing themselves from a manufacturer of rubber to cell phones. When people who've lost a leg or an arm still manage to let go of who they used to be and reinvent themselves in order to run for the Paralympic Games, we're amazed. At the other end of the scale, it's kind of shabby when your boss, colleague, friend or a family member refuses to recognize a new reality that's right in front of them. Instead they become increasingly more agitated.

The boss, who sees that the market has changed, but instead of seizing the day and take on the challenge, s/he continues the routine of planning more meetings and setting up new guidelines followed by a lot of talk about the need for the employees to do something new, so that the C-level bosses can maintain the status quo.

Sigh!

The colleague, who didn't move with the times and didn't attend to his or her network, didn't train further and improve her skill set, and who is now first in line in the upcoming round of layoffs. And who still believes it's underserving, because she really worked hard for ten straight years, blah, blah, blah.

Sigh!

The friend, who powers ahead on bicycle or at ultra-runs, because he can't stand being at home nor in his own shell due to an overload of personal issues that even his issues have issues.

Sigh!

Mom and dad, who have become increasingly annoyed with their teenager, because deep down they're grieving for the chubby baby he used to be and whom some spotted kid with smelly feet ate.

Sigh!

Your best piece of advice aimed at the pessimists and doomsayers should be this: Take responsibility for what's yours whether it weighs one gram or one tonne. Ask the universe for recognition. Lean into the discomfort of the irritation and let it fill you up. For when you do, things will be so much more fun.

A friend of ours was driving with his teenage daughter. At one point the girl looks at him and asks, "Dad, I wonder where all the idiots are when Mom is driving?"

The future will come to those who make room for it. The ones who dare letting go of their shit. It hurts saying goodbye to the ego, old status, to the ideal you never achieved, but the payoff compares favorably with the pain.

So, let's instead dig deeper into the mind and have a look at what's happening with your brains, when you are annoyed, and why acceptance is the key to pretty much all the locked doors you'll meet on your way.

Cognitive Dissonance – When the World Is Plain Stupid!

In 1957, the American psychologist, Leon Festinger, proposed a theory on cognitive dissonance. 'Cognition' means recognition, while 'dissonance' means disagreement.

When reality moves, you either read it like it is and achieve cognitive resonance, or you read it like you think it is, for which you'll achieve cognitive dissonance – a little thing we like to call 'irritation.' Your perception of reality is clashing with what's actually going on and the brain experiences this as extreme discomfort.

This is why the brain gets to work and tries to maintain some sort of concordance between your thoughts and ideas on the one side and your actual behavior on the other. Meaning, you either stretch for reality or try to bend it to fit with your story about reality.

The Future Is Constantly on the Move

Bending reality for your own purposes is hard work. Firstly, because it's so much bigger than you. And secondly, because it's a scientific fact that the universe is growing and that our recognition and understanding of the world is always falling behind. The universe also becomes more and more messy. It's called entropy.

Order can usually only exist in a few ways, while disorder (or chaos) might have billions and billions of outcomes. There's only one final solution to a jigsaw puzzle, while the false way continues indefinitely. The wire to your recharger gets entangled with your earphones, the cabinet doors in the kitchen fall off, everything gets worn down – disorder will accumulate no matter what you do, it's not your fault. By natural law, all things decay and turn into something less structured and disorganized.

The more you have to control, the messier and more chaotic it will be.

Shut the Fuck Up!

Every single day you become annoyed. A series of nagging problems keeps repeating itself, but what does it really mean?

Annoying kids
Kids are usually annoying because they are overly excited. And they make a mess. Plus, they're constantly trying to suck the energy out of us. Stupid little love vampires...

Hidden message: Okay, so you're annoyed because your kids are laughing and having fun and want to be with you? And because they're living in the now and love to play? Alrighty then...

Annoying employees and bosses
They're often annoying because they talk too much, don't deliver or don't appreciate us enough... or they don't know what they're talking about?

Hidden message: Do you need to put down your foot and mark a boundary? Are you being too nice? Maybe you should be the boss, so why don't you chase the position? Are they maybe trying to tell you to be less the pleaser and more no-nonsense? Are people not seeing you because you don't let them? Are they asking for more than you can actually deliver?

Traffic
You're not stuck in traffic. You are traffic. To some people, traffic jam, holding still or being slowed down is like dying a slow death. Result? Road rage!

Hidden message: Standing still is a possibility for your internal agency to catch up on you. In this case, it always almost means that there's something in your life you don't like, or that you don't really know where you're headed. Maybe you should be doing something completely different? Listen louder! Your soul is trying to tell you something you already know.

In order to be able to actually being in the chaos that is reality, human beings have used stories to create structure and order. Usually, the stories were unfounded in reality so as to better focus on the things that supported the order that decision makers so desired. With fewer pieces at hand, it was easier to keep track of. The more pieces to the puzzle of history there are, the more wacky it will seem. In the old days, people believed in witches, elfs and trolls. One myth narrates the story of trolls, who were transformed into rocks if they didn't reach their caves by dawn. Another is concerned with infants suffering from colic or some other condition that caused a change in behavior. They were seen as 'changelings,' a troll had exchanged them with a kid from Hell. This was a way of making sense of the fact that all of a sudden there was a huge rock in your field that wasn't there yesterday or that there was a reason why baby John started screaming madly.

To modern and fairly rational people, stories about changelings and trolls seem a little quirky. But, when you live in a village and speak with the same people about more or less the same things day after day and then something new and dramatic happens, it calls for an explanation. And that explanation is rarely based on the most recent science or reasonable front line research. The explanation is based on the most exciting (or most scary) story that can be made up to fit with the occasion.

Stories have always created a calm, safety and meaning in our chaos. And you know what? It's perfectly okay, because stories explain the connection between the present, the past and the future. The only thing we shouldn't do is believing that our stories (explanations) are the reality.

For there are as many realities as there are people on earth. It's not a coincidence that the Renaissance began in Italy, where traveling merchants, manufacturers, seafarers and a multitude of languages, religion and cultures were plenty.

When a lot of stories clash in a room, where there's an interest
in creating something new, all sorts of things can happen – we're
updating the software of the brain and go down in history as the ones
who saw it coming, the ones who seized the opportunity.

Out Here on the Edge

Your reality will always be more or less limited than the actual reality
and the future. Unless, of course, you are God.

**The Future is
Expanding.**
*The small orange circle
illustrates your recognition
of the world. It's your story
about who you are, what you
know, and what you are able
to do.*

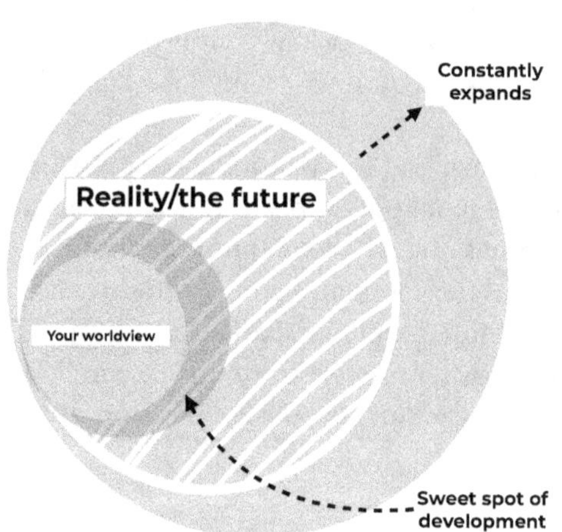

You experience cognitive resonance and dissonance every single day
in the world around you. Here on the edge of your worldview, where
your recognition collides with the actual reality, irritation arises.

When you're resonating, your recognition of the world matches the
reality. You'll make good decisions, read the traffic right, you spot
the trends in good time before the wave hits and adjust accordingly.
You'll park you car where you don't get a ticket. You'll know that
wearing swimwear at the beach is okay, but not in the grocery store.
And people will laugh when you tell jokes, and they'll appreciate the
presents you give.

If you're experiencing cognitive dissonance, your prospect and world view is out of sync. Like a computer running on old software. We update the software in our computers, because new things are happening and we want accordance with what's going on out there and what our computers are able to do.

The Growth Mindset, the Fixed Mindset and the Futurist Mindset

If your story about who you are is that you're a lifelong learner, who's always in process and are never done working on yourself, and if you're willing to experiment and are ready to accept putting up with irritation and recognize the wisdom of others, you're not fighting against reality. You'll meet and shape it as good as you can. Your worldview is expanding and in spite of the chaos and unrest in your immediate surroundings, you'll experience peace at heart, in your brain and in your stomach.

In her book 'Mindset,' the American professor at Stanford University, Carol Dweck, terms this 'the growth mindset.'

A person with a 'fixed mindset' equates who they are with what they do. Where a student with a 'growth mindset' will think that the paper or project got a grade and they'll use that to do better next time, a student with a 'fixed mindset' will think, "I got a bad grade, therefore I suck."

If you lock up your perception of reality and let your ego and identity run the show, the world is bound to be extremely annoying. Take John McEnroe, the tennis player. A huge talent, who managed to stage the most embarrassing acts in the court, when reality (from the view of the head judge) was not on his side. Like McEnrow, the fixed mindset is not an impediment to success.

The problem is that your recognition will not be expanded, because the wall between your ego and the surroundings is way too high. And you'll waste an opportunity to use your energy on something that could actually release great things in the world.

The world is full of people with blazing cognitive dissonance, whose bitter response toward the new and different is to maintain their ego and what they know, as if the stakes were life itself (which is what it will feel like to them). And they'll maintain this view point even though it doesn't work for them at all and their everyday life stinks. We all now people beyond pedagogical reach, who don't have the desire nor the energy to consider the facts or listen to reasoned arguments.

We know them, because they are us, too. So why are we annoyed with other people, when they try to escape reality? We are, because deep down, behind the taboos, we know that we, too, are guilty of running away from them.

"Can't you see?" we yell at each other.

But you can only see if you're willing to look.

Luckily, when you are preoccupied by the cognitive tasks of a higher order, this is the point where you're able to see the world and reality as well as the future with other eyes than your own. This is where your future brain is dancing the samba.

Holding on to your story is comparable to holding your breath. In the beginning, it feels okay. But in time, you'll be choking. You must let go and exhale in order to breathe in the fresh air. And when you let go of the old stuff, you give it the chance of revival.

The same goes for the story about yourself. It's only strong and viable if it's also bendable and flexible. 'Standing your ground' and 'being ready for change' are not opposite sides to the same story. They are each other's prerequisites. Let reality in the same way you take a deep breath. Exhale, breathe in. Let go of the old convictions and spend your energy on refreshing the things that are important.

When you use your irritation in this way, you'll be super fit for the future.

Alternative Facts

People, who are raised in the scientific belief, can be ever so furious and offended that 'fake news' are spreading at the speed of light. They use all of their energy to speak ill of people, who are prone to listen to gossip and urban legends. And they dream nostalgically about the time, when the whole world got their news from the same newspapers.

It's in our nature to seek the company of those who hold the same views as we do, and we'll cultivate the stories about how important we are, while we look down upon the stupidity of the mob and become increasingly frustrated with the state of the world.

However, if people adhering to the scientific belief would only listen a little louder to their own irritation, they would have to start by acknowledging reality as it is. Only then will it be possible to ask uncomfortable questions like, "Did we, the self-imposed clever ones, forget to create a forum, where those who don't have a higher education and are not very good at joggling academia can join in? Did we act the part of the bully and overcomplicate the public debate to the point of smugness? Can trolling, feeling offended, yelling and gossiping perhaps also be seen as different forms of debate?"

In short: Accept that people don't adhere to the facts! If you don't accept it, you'll be swallowing the same bait that you're accusing other people of – arguing on account of your own feelings.

Use Your Intuition to Explore the Future and Do Misunderstand What You See

The evolutionary history of mankind is predominantly made up of experiments, misunderstandings and – KAMBOOM! – woops, something just exploded. Let's call it gun powder. We'll venture into an experiment and create something only to destroy it again and then we explain what happened afterward.

In science, this is called hypotheses and this is what real futurological research is about. In working with the hypothesis, we're being curious, asking great questions and playing around with thoughts like: "Imagine if…"

A hypothesis is a scenario that encourages you to venture into a project, gather the funding necessary and hire people because you want to create something that doesn't yet exist. When in 1955, the game changer, Joseph Salk, inoculated 1,8 million American kids against polio, it was the end of a seven year long journey, which none of his colleagues at the universities had supported, much less believed in.

Salk sought and got private funding for chasing a cure for a disease, which, at this point in time, Americans were as afraid of as nuclear war. Later on, Salk said, "My attitude was always to keep open, to keep scanning. I think that's how things work in nature. Many people are close-minded, rigid, and that's not my inclination."

It should be noted that a lot of his former … *ahem* narrow-minded *ahem* colleagues found Salk extremely annoying. A lot of them also envied the rock star status that he earned in this endeavor, when standing applause in airplanes and hotel upgrades became an everyday thing for him.

If we look back and take a closer look at the history of the world, we've had far more break throughs in times, when resources, tools and knowledge were much more scarce than they are today. Modern research has so much knowledge, time, money, international network, artificial intelligence, incredible machines and tools at its disposal. Still, the return on investments made in science is declining. Why that is nobody can actually say, but one of the reasons could be that the hypotheses are too certain and also too close to 'reality.' We are far less willing to take risks and need to double check everything inside out (and again with HR), which means that so much creative energy is spend on upgrading existing products like medicine or platforms to new versions, which will maintain patients and serve as an explanation for increased price levels.

Another reason is that the social climate in scientific circles typically isn't very motivating and appreciative in relation to thinking outside the box and generating wacky gaga ideas, let alone saying these things out loud. There simply isn't room for rebels in science anymore, while 'cake and foosball' for all the lemmings is plenty. Besides this internal bickering, the scientific community suffers under an enormous pressure to publish research articles and being peer-reviewed by others. The point of it all is of course to create a fundamental framework for solid and recognized research, but in reality, it often ends up as a defensive waiting game, where everyone holds their arms very tight to the body.

As a futurist, you are part of a community, which is dedicated to create the safe room of curiosity, where our storytelling brains can relax and become infused with other people's thoughts, ideas and ways of doing things. Places, where we feel like opening up to the many trends we see knocking on our gates in the present. You'll invite a new and global Renaissance into existence, where the village is no longer a place, but a mindset. And in that process, we can't avoid irritation.

Luckily, because…

Irritation And Magic Are Two Sides of the Same Coin

This is our rule of thumb:

- Irritation will tell you that you're standing on the 'wrong side' of history, that you've got the wrong vantage point.
- Magic occurs, when you're standing on the 'right side' of history. You're the hero of the game and has chosen wisely and with insight.

In Steven Spielberg's movie, 'Raiders of the Lost Ark' (1981), Indiana Jones is the hero, who is chased through the streets of Cairo by a bunch of bad guys. He runs through a market place and ends up in a square face to face with a very scary swordsman, who laughs and throws his weapon from hand to hand preparing for what appears to be an epic duel of the whip and the sword. Instead, Indiana shoots the swordsman.

Magic!

Later on, Harrison Ford, who starred in Indiana Jones, said that this scene indeed was planned as a duel. But due to a severe case of indigestion, he was only able to shoot bits of ten minutes at a time, before he had to run off to the loo in his trailer. The scene was set to take three days to shoot, and Ford thought really long and hard about how he was going to get out of it. So, he suggested to Spielberg that he could just shoot the guy. And the rest is history.

By the way, the lost fight of swords is a brilliant example of a game changer: The swordsman thought it was about these 'rules we agreed on,' and then the game changed to something else.

Those of us who identify with the hero standing on the 'right side' of history experience this as a moment of magic and truly funny. But for the guy with the sword standing on the 'wrong side' of history, it's an extremely annoying situation. A fun fact for movie lovers is that the swordsman in reality was a phenomenal and really talented British stuntman, who had practiced his skills for months before this shoot. No wonder he didn't laugh as hard that his character got shot instead.

So, if the future and reality are magical things in your world, keep doing what you do. If they are annoying, then stop and think for a moment. Could it be that you're being the bad guy? Are you standing on the wrong side of history? Is your vantage point annoying? Then let it go and start looking for the magic.

This rule of thumb is not 100% water proof, but it's enough for you to navigate with.

Level 4
THE GAME
CHANGER

YOU BECOME THE FUTURE YOU SPOT

Chapter 7
You Become the Future You Spot

As a futurist, one of your most important tasks is to predict trends, which means being able to sense a vibe or a movement in society or predicting the way people behave. A trend can be anything from the dominance of hip hop in music, to the wave of paleo we saw in the 2010s, to crossfit as a type of workout. It can be the wave of freedom that sweeps across the world overthrowing dictatorships, the sudden increase of suicide rates or the dissociation from expensive products or air travel.

A trend is a development, a movement or an observation with a potential to transform and change the ways in which we think, feel, work, consume or experience the world.

The many drops of ideas and creations, which eventually make the wave that collides with other waves and turns into an eternal whirlpool of motion is a great metaphor for understanding the dynamics of the trends that shape both the present and the future as well as the past. Like water, trends are in constant motion, and as soon as you catch them, you have to let them go again. In the same way, the future is not something you must struggle to understand, before you have to do something with it. It would be the same as if you drank the entire ocean before you went for a swim.

Trends as Photos and Movies

Imagine that you're standing on a beach and take a photo. You've not captured an image of the coastline, the ripples in the water, the small crab at your feet … you've caught reality in a frame at a certain point in time.

If you take a photo of yourself, you focus on the motive and what captivates you in that moment. That's a vantage point. As a player in the Game of the Future, your perspective is changing. In that very same photo, you'll be able to spot several trends if you look for plastic on the beach, which says something about the way the world handles resources. Maybe there's a party in the background with young people dancing around with water bottles instead of alcohol, and … wait a minute. There are also some older guests there, which makes you ponder on old age no longer being what it was. Also, did you use a single-use camera to take the photo, or did you use your cell phone or a drone? Is there an element of surprise in the background that you didn't notice before?

No matter where you stand and no matter where you're looking, you will see trends. A simple light switch will tell you the story about the time when fire was our only source of light in the dark. Then we made expensive candles made of wax, followed by oil lamps and incandescent bulbs and with it the (very meaning full) idea of bringing light to the people. Few people are interested in the technological products per se. It's what the light bulb does, you know, the fact that we can also work in the dark that we pay for. And with that trend, the growing need of working and producing more hours a day, General Motors was born. Today, light switches have become much more elegant and durable, and it won't be long before they become smart switches that can adjust and customize the lumen and lux to the people in the room. Light has the the potential to become the wi-fi of the future, and car lights will be able to monitor distances in traffic. "Well, well, aha, interesting," right? Right! And then what happens? We don't know, but it will be an exciting adventure to find out. Will light be able to help us work, not more, but better? More intelligently?

A trend doesn't have to be as big a break through as Edison and his light bulb in order to be significant. Trends can be little ripples in the surface that catch your attention, but which in reality is just a craze coming and going. They can sneak in on you without you noticing, you can surf the wave without having a sense of direction and they can be tsunamis changing the status quo. You'll still drink coffee, go to work and watch the news, but the way and the quality of how it reaches you will be permanently changed over time. Some things improved, others didn't, and most of it, we forgot. That's just the way it is.

Take a look at the world around you and feel how everything is constantly moving, including the things that seem eternal and unalterable. Kids are still playing, but they play with completely different things than kids 100 years ago. We're still listening to music, but the music reaches our ears in a completely different manner than just 10 years ago. Bank robbers are still a thing in this world, but if they weren't able to read the trends and still robbed banks like they did in the 80's (balaclava, guns, escape vehicles and all), they would be ridiculed. Everything has to change in order for everything to remain the same, and those who see the future and get their fingers out are the ones, who (on average) do better than the ones, who fight nail and tooth to defend the past.

If in a year or so, you take out your photo of the beach and look at it, the motive will still look like a real beach. But the fact remains that the real beach will be completely different from the beach on your photo. There will not be a grain of sand, a wave or a person like on your photo. Entropy always alters the shape and look of things. Something new came along, something disappeared and a lot of things still look the same. It's just somewhere else.

Play With the Shutter Speed

With a little technological ingenuity you can expose the movements. A camera can be set with either fast or slow shutter speeds. A fast shutter speed will produce a very precise image that shows no movement. A slow shutter speed will give you a blurred focus, but the motive reveals that things are moving from something to something else.

In physics and math, it's known as the 'Heisenberg uncertainty principle:' You can't both measure the exact location of an object (for instance a football or a car) and then also accurately measure where it's headed. If you want to know exactly where the object is, you have to pin it down or freeze it. If you want to know how it moves, you can't really say exactly. It's a case of either or. For everything is relative. Everything is connected and impacts each other.

The same goes for trends. For you as a futurist, the point is fundamentally that your goal in trend spotting isn't to get it right or being accurate. Your goal is the ability to see something before it happens, to predict, sense and set the direction in a world that seems more and more chaotic and uncertain. A world, which after all still has certain constant rules and principles to lean on.

If you describe your trends like a single photo, like a concept a la 'disruption,' 'globalization,' 'urbanization,' 'gamification,' 'digitization,' 'core service,' 'artificial intelligence,' 'sustainability,' or 'protectionism,' you'll only capture a status update. The sense of what the trend actually means to the transformation of your world and how you can use it to make the best possible decision will not be in it. You will lose the movement.

What's even worse, these trend spots, these single points of impact, are often used to scare people off: The refugee crisis is NOW! We're all disrupted NOW! Artificial Intelligence will take over all of our jobs NOW! Biodiversity goes down the drain NOW! It compares to you standing in the waterline with a single focus on the one shark far out in the ocean, who'll probably eat you, if you go further out into the water. Remember from the previous levels, that you make incredibly lousy decisions, when you are afraid. Always return to the neutral "well, well." You're not supposed to drink the ocean, just step into it!

The really good players in the Game of the Future are not satisfied with stills and single shots captured with a specific shutter speed. They want to capture photos using both slow and fast shutter speeds and they make movies. A piece of advice from all of us to all of you: Don't just narrow your focus to one image, one idea about the future, or one trend. A movie is made up of a lot of images that move so fast that our brains perceive them as flow. So when you go trend spotting, you have to spot a lot of trends (as in A LOT of trends) and piece them together into a movie – your movie – about the future, including scenarios, ideas and visions.

It's really not that different from the practice of athletes. Like the ice hockey player, Wayne Gretzky, said when he was asked why he was so good, "A good hockey player plays where the puck is. A great hockey player plays where the puck is going to be." You must think like Gretzky, and look at the world, not just as you are, but as it is. You also need to see the world for what it might become and then go there, using your gut feeling, heart, your business and your magic moments to navigate with.

Science is helping the best athletes in the world to become even better. And no, we're not thinking forbidden drugs here. Athletes are constantly analyzing their training, patterns of movement, their diet and their poodoo. But in the end, sports is not a scientific endeavor. Scientific results can go a long way, but at the end of the day, the athlete will be competing under circumstances that cannot be controlled – the weather, the opponent, sleep, just to mention a few. All are unknown factors.

The same goes for the Game of the Future. Futurology is an eclectic (a fancy word for borrowing a little here and there) and not an exact approach. If, however, you do need to be specific and accurate in your trend spotting, you will have a hard time seeing the movements. Plus, your audience will not have room to play and experiment. If you only open the door to the creative universe, where everything is fluid and in flow, you'll get a great feeling about it, but you'll have a hard time explaining exactly what it is you're seeing.

From Something to Something Else

When you're trend spotting, you need to collect observations with the purpose of looking for transformations: Where is the trend coming from and where is it heading?

Describe your trend as a movement: from something to something else. The trend behind digitization, for instance, is "from analog to digital."

The trend behind traffic jam on the highway could be "from transport to mobility."

A provoking trend for the trade union movement would be "from retained to released."

Your trends must never be normative, they have to come across as clear and self-evident so that later on, they can be mapped or connected with other trends. It's not until they are placed within a larger framework that new patterns, scenarios and interesting invitations to radical change emerge.

One of the advantages by describing trends as transformations (from something to something else) is that one idea doesn't exclude the other. When we talk about 'digitization,' people tend to believe that EVERYTHING needs to be digitalized. But the trend only refers to the fact that what used to be analogue is now moving in a digital direction. In other sectors or industries, the trend might be moving in a different direction, and so the things we don't want to see digitalized (like the empathetic relation between teachers and students or practitioners and patients) we can in fact decide to amplify analogically. The future has room for a lot of things. Yes, a lot of jobs and stuff will eventually disappear or become outdated, but the things that have value to us will eventually find their place. To a futurist, coexistence is much more common and natural than competition. After all, we're still using pencils even though we've got the ball point pen and the keyboard.

Trend Spotting – Keep It Simple

A photographer can make use of different filters, Photoshop and editing tools that will enhance and change the expression of a photograph. To you, it would be like applying emotions like anxiety or mountaineering, a political opinion or personal assessment to your trends. This is an absolute no-go if you're a futurist. You have to aim for observations that come across as raw, naked and unedited impressions. The more neutral and objective you can be with regard to your motive, the more interesting and real you will be to collaborate with. People generally see through your 'picture perfect,' which means you're only interesting for a very small group of people, who believe the same as you.

We've talked a lot about taking pictures of trends and that is one of the things you can do. With a physical camera that is. But you need to know that as a futurist, you must always observe the world around you, which is why you need to teach your brain to 'take a lot of mental pictures' that you can describe afterward. Your observations can be 'real' motives like the beach, but it can also be moods and atmospheres, emotions, new ways of solving problems, a thought, an idea, a hypothesis or an imagined widget or solution to a problem. Just suck everything in and say, "Well, well, aha, interesting." Fill out your note books, for the more impressions you can feed your predictive brain, the more data it will have to process in its predictions. If it's full of observations, in time, it will be natural for you to come out as a visionary.

So. Once again: Be curious, let in the light and stop overthinking as you explore the future. As you know, the brain prefers organizing everything in relation to the things you know already, and if you fall into that trap, you run the risk of creating too many blind spots.

The Game Changer-Trends of the Future Zoom In on You

The most important thing about trend spotting is to be awake and curious about the world. Basically, it all about getting started. You can't walk on water without getting your pants wet. Trend spotting is fun! And the techniques we give you will support you in the process and not increase the complexity.

> **Don'ts:** Asking questions and overanalyzing everything you see to assess whether or not it's important or not. Also, don't draw conclusions too soon.

> **Dos:** Open up. Say, "Welcome to my brain, knock yourself out while you collect new, funny, quirky, annoying, and inspiring input." Embrace the mess.

When you hunt for trends, sooner or later you will find your game changer. A game changer is the trend that makes the future zoom in on you and you'll be like: "If this is what's going to happen, it will definitely change the rules of the game." As you play the Game of the Future, you will stumble upon other trends that are relevant to you. But you might experience that they will align to fit with your game changer and help you move on. Your game changer will help build new communities and destroy some of the old and invite radical changes that only people with an attuned MBS, future sense and respect for each other's principles will be able to effectuate. As the name implies, game changers change the rules of the game. Your game changer will be annoying, but it will also represent the magic of the future.

Throughout history many futurists were killed (completely knocked down) for finding their game changer and following their vocation. They changed the game and created new stories. They became the game changer.

If you create your own stories and change the game, you will simultaneously change the power structures that uphold the old system, which means the old players will come to get you.

The scientist Galileo Galilei (1564-1642) proved that Earth orbits the sun. And then the Vatican threw him in jail. Edward Snowden revealed several cases of large-scale surveillance in the US, and then he took flight to Russia. Martin Luther King Jr. (1929-1968) worked to rebel against racism in the USA. And he got shot. History is littered with the dead bodies of famous as well as unknown futurists and game changers.

You earn bonus points when you get the old players to cross the bridge instead of fighting them. Do you see how they're rumbling with Tribal and are stuck in the past, that their taboos prevent them from crossing the bridge to the future and that they have a hard time letting go of their vantage point?

They need a new story about the future to take example from, the encouragement to be more than just a tourist.

Their ability to visualize things has dried out, because it stands on the shoulders of the past and because they use their creative powers to maintain the status quo. To them, the future is a dangerous place, very scary. Your job is to use your vision and the creative powers that you've obtained throughout the game to make them see the magic in their own game changers.

There are many types of trends, the most important are 'hard trends,' 'soft trends,' and of course the 'game changers.' If you're presenting trends or are arguing the case for a movement you see, it's important that you know the different types of trends. When you're doing the actual research, you don't have to think about it. Here, you'll just need to keep open and stay in the "Well, well, aha, interesting"-tourist mode.

Later on in the book, we will give you an outline and description of the most important trends.

Level 5
THE SEVEN DEMONS

DON'T SWALLOW THE BAIT, KEEP YOUR ENERGY LEVELS HIGH AND STAY FOCUSED

The Piss Ant
The Procrastinator
Stormtroopers
The Eraser
The Dark Demon
Complex Rex
The Humping Troll

Chapter 8

Don't swallow the bait, keep your energy levels high and stay focused

"Beware that, when fighting monsters, you yourself do not become a monster... for when you gaze long enough into the abyss, the abyss will gaze back into you." (Friedrich Nietzsche)

In the Game of the Future, you will stand face to face with several demons that you meet along the way. They're running back and forth between Tribal and Planetary and they're on a frightening quest: to disturb and make you confused and doubt yourself and your mission. They'll stick to your body like parasites draining you for resources, especially time, focus, energy and trust.

To put it differently: the demons want you to take part in the wrong story, so that you forget all about being a future warrior fighting for love, empathy and kindness.

You attract your demons for a reason. They are designed to be annoying, to dazzle you and tear up your wounds and traumas. It's painful as hell, but the payoff is that they present a golden opportunity to have look at yourself from a 360 degree perspective, to heal and move up in levels in the game as well as consciously.

An emphatic person wants to save everyone, but beware! Demons love to tear things apart, destroy and twist for no reason what so ever.

Demons get their powers mainly because you think that they think like you.

Or, because you mistake them for being poor creatures in want of a little TLC.

Demons are a burden you absolutely don't carry with a smile. Instead, you should give them a circular kick in the balls, right where it hurts, when they come hunting for you and your buddy.

In order to give you the best options to hit the bull's eye, you need to know who your opponents are.

So, Ladies and Gentlemen: Introducing the seven demons in the Game of the Future…

The Dark Demon

The Dark Demon is evil. He is the most powerful demon of them all, as he resides inside of you in the form of that little dark and ghosty voice that whispers poison in your ear. He is the shadow and the darkness, the evil thoughts from the darkest depths of your soul. He is the one telling you that you're not good enough, talented enough, that you're being fake, too pleased with yourself, that you're unreliable and that everyone is laughing at you behind your back. He'll tell you that someone will expose you, that you're all alone in the world and that nobody loves you. He'll laugh at you waltzing around making false pretences. The Dark Demon doesn't wish you well. At all. "In fact," as Marianne Williamson, Deepak Chopra and Debbie Ford write in their book 'The Shadow Effect,' "it is the part of you that wants to see you dead."

The Dark Demon is that part of all of us that makes us unconsciously act evil toward ourselves, toward others, toward the planet. Carl Jung (1875-1961), the psychiatrist, referred to him as 'the Shadow.' The Dark Demon doesn't not want you to know that he's there. His primary interest is to make you believe that he is you.

Throughout your life, the Dark Demon will be an unwanted passenger on your train ride to the future. He will always be ugly and someone to be ashamed of, and you will want to hide him. He wants you to have a depression or suffer from anxiety and isolate yourself.

Don't do that!

The best way to defeat the Dark Demon is to confront him 'face to face' empowered by love and bring him into the light, where he'll slowly wither as you seize the magic of the future and make peace with your shortcomings. When you open your basement door to have a look at the survey of your fundament, you're bound to find a shit load of crap. And the longer you hesitate to deal with it, the more it will stink. But remember, shit is nothing more than a fertilizer for your soul and your humaneness.

The people who love you can easily see that you keep a treasury of taboos and traumas. They're only waiting for the moment when you're ready to open up so they can finally help you.

One of the things that define us the most is the company we keep, the people we surround ourselves and spend time with. So, are you relations dark or light? Maybe it's time you gave them a little shake? The Dark Demon will lose his hold of you when you finally accept your weaknesses and allow other people to care for you just as you are with all your faults. And if they don't, they're not your true friends.

Always speak to yourself as if you were your best friend. You deserve nothing less! One MBS-trick that works wonders for us is to say this phrase out loud every time the Dark Demon shows his ugly face: "Right! I will now express my will to look at myself or this thing in a different light!" Take a short break, talk to someone and look at yourself from their perspective. And then laugh a little at yourself, each other and all the stupid thoughts we're all struggling to come to terms with. Humor is light, joy and a sign of intelligent thinking, and when we reach the point when we can actually laugh at the Dark Demon, we've come a long way.

The Humping Troll

Don't mistake the Humping Troll for the odious and frightening Taboo Troll. The Humping Troll is constantly on the attack, but he's not very brave. Social media is his preferred arena and he will send vicious and insinuating comments your way in the form of petty and small-minded personal attacks. His favorite weapons are coincidence and vanity. Coincidence, as there is no deeper meaning behind choosing you as his victim. It might as well be somebody else. And vanity, because this demon will poke at your supposed lack of qualities or attribute opinions to you that you don't agree with or never in a million years would say. If you're afraid of being 'exposed' or you don't feel 'clever enough,' rest assured that he will use those very arguments against you. On the bright side, a visit from the Humping Troll means you'll most likely identify a wound that needs to be healed, and you do so by giving yourself the recognition you expect from others. People who are at peace with their faults and are okay with not having a 'proper education' or the 'perfect qualifications for the job,' don't pay attention to comments like these, right?

A typical attack from the Humping Troll is a scattering of arguments that doesn't relate to the content you published at all. His trick is to accuse you of something completely off track, which makes your blood boil and compels you to snap back. Another trick of his is to attack your premise and the ground you're standing on, your vision and the things you believe in, which most often is our soft spot, the area where we're all skating on thin ice. For example, we once saw a professor of economics, who was out on a limb because the students in his class wouldn't accept the premise of 'X' as an unknown quantity (yes, the scene unfolded in a Political Science class).

If you look closer, you'll see that there really is no higher meaning with this demon's attack, none whatsoever. Starting a hare in a debate, sucking up all the attention and wasting your time is more than enough for him.

In the TV-show 'Friends,' Phoebe makes fun of Ross, who's a palaeontologist, researcher and dinosaur fan. Having dry humped poor Ross for a while, she nonchalantly shrugs her shoulders, "That was fun! So, who's hungry?"

Your defence against the demons is to ignore them: "Don't feed the trolls," as the saying goes.

But deep down you want to win the fight so badly that you try your best to call on reason, common sense and your sense of justice. Know, however, that it's impossible to argue your way to victory in the face of this nasty fellow. Typically, you'll see 20 or so battles back and forth, before one of you calls the other one a Nazi. And all the while, the horny little thing is busy dry humping your leg with his little devil dick and groaning with delight.

Picture that! The Humping Troll in the act of dry humping you all covered in chili and hot chocolate sauce. The more energy, words and attention you throw at this demon, the more satisfied the horny, little devil will be.

Don't take it personally, though. Shake him off, literally, like a dog. One of the reasons why animals shake their bodies is to get rid of nervous energy. The same applies for human beings.

Remember, the best weapon to fight a demon is to use humor. Especially when it's disguised as facts (with a touch of threats). James Blunt, the musician, is phenomenal at fighting back demons on Twitter. Take this tweet, for instance, "I wanna go see James Blunt so I can call him a faggot and throw a soda at him." To which James Blunt replies (on Twitter), "I'm on a US tour now. Tickets available online." Or this one, "Omfg James Blunt is on the TV downstairs, can this day get any worse!" James Blunt: "Coming upstairs now."

In a thread, a reader once made an epic snap attack in reply to
a condescending comment about Jews, women and people with
disabilities, saying quite simply: "Hitler… is that you?"

This kind of chivalry is a powerful weapon. If you read a great article
online and discover that the writer gets dry humped from left and
right, then pitch in with your perspective and knock down the demon
humpers. "The pen is mightier than the sword," as the British writer
Edward Bulwer-Lytton wrote in 1839. You can have an amazing
experience fighting off someone else's Humping Troll.

It's also possible to run into a Humper in meatspace, but, like we said,
they're not very brave, so they're not likely to confront you there. The
Humping Troll in the work space will defame you behind your back
and twist someone's message, and they just love it if we get drunk or
do embarrassing things at the Christmas party. The more attention
you pay to them, the more powerful they become. The best defence?
Ignore them, use humor to deflate their balloon and show chivalry on
behalf of others. Remember that the Humping Troll prods quick and
hard, but the wounds heal fast. Don't take it personally, it's not worth
it.

P.S. If you're the team lead and have a Humper in your group,
remember to spook him every now and then, "Booooo!" If the culture
is lacking some neighborly love, it's time to toughen up and revisit your
code of conduct.

Stormtroopers

It's not easy to make eye contact with the Stormtroopers. It's impossible to get them to recognize that their behavior is not okay. Everything is always someone else's fault. When it's just the two of you, they can be your best friend and act super nice. But in the company of others, they'll turn on a dime.

Stormtroopers will never make a move on their own, and a real trooper always believes the same as the group majority. Their weapon is adult bullying and group pressure. They fall into the categories of 'stupid' and 'big power.' If you try to reach them with enlightening information and great arguments, you'll be just as successful as if you tried to stop a horde of cattle by reading out loud the rules of good etiquette. In our younger days, we did a workshop for a management group. And holy moly, did we work hard to please them. They were all hungry for a tête-à-tête with us, where they fervently wanted to share their dreams and hopes for the future, their innermost deepest thoughts about their suffering and frustrations, careers, private lives, teenagers and so on. That night, the party was on and people were engaged in really deep conversations about the future, so we went to bed with a great feeling, "Wow, this is going so well!" Before wrapping it up the next day, the moderator did a round table to let everyone have a say and evaluate the work we had done. Warning: Everything crashed. The baby died!

At first, they were all very quiet, and then one after another they began talking about how irrelevant, complex, abstract and academic it had all been. A quiet whisper spread throughout the room, while the visors of the stormtroopers lowered to cut off all human contact and empathy.

We sat in the corner, while the walls of the waste shaft on the Death Star slowly closed and our only hope of salvation was to be flushed down the drain with the rest of the trash.

During this seance, we caught the eye of the guy, who had been the most ecstatic and enthusiastic the night before and who had said things like, "This stuff is life changing!" Great, so we'll at least have one life line, we thought. Nope. We did not! He quickly looked the other way and joined the choir. What went wrong? Did we really suck?

The moderator, who to this day remains a good friend and client, said to us: "Listen up. You guys are young (true, we were), clever and super talented. And you're presenting a future that they know deep down they have to be able to navigate. But they don't understand shit. They just realized that they've hit rock bottom and have to start all over again. Today, they're returning to a reality that has no room for innovation and excitement, and so it's so much easier for them to agree that you guys are the ones, who are not good enough. Instead of owning their story and taking responsibility for implementing the necessary changes, they lean on the things they know – and turn against you. They give up before they've even started." Thank you very much, friend!

So, after 48 hours and a good six bottles of red wine later, we crawled out of our tortoise shells. This is how long it typically takes a futurist to rise after a stormtrooper attack.

Group dynamics are not rational. When the visor is up and the helmet is off, it's easy to feel connected with a stormtrooper, but you never know where you got them. The stormtrooper is rooted in the part of the human mind that can be programmed according to the lowest common denominator, the part of us that wants to believe the same as everyone else, camp followers and gregarious animals. Possessed by this demon, we can all become stupid and dangerous 'flying monkeys.' Especially, when you're playing in Tribal. Big is the person, who dares to stand his or her ground.

Your defence against the Stormtroopers is first and foremost to stand firm on your core beliefs. Listen to your own words. When are you doing the talking and when are you hearing voices from the past and old programs you adapted from others? Listen carefully to your three brains. Another way of going about it is to study chief executives and politicians on TV. You can train your ability to hearing and seeing. Notice the difference when they talk about things they really care about and mean themselves and when they're really just rabbling off a (party) program. Being a good human being is hard. Especially in these sellout times, in the transition between the Tribal and the Planetary mode, where in the short run, it pays off to be opportunistic and line your pockets. But just because other people act like idiots, you don't have to.

See it as an opportunity for you to use your sense of humor as a unique sword: Stormtroopers love imbecile jokes and they'll go to great lengths for a cup of coffee, breakfast rolls and cookies. They love to 'shit chat' and are often very kind and vulnerable human beings, who are not very good at showing up as themselves.

So it all amounts to this: Stormtroopers, having listened to all of your many words and plans, will usually say that they don't see it. No wonder you can't see it, you're wearing a helmet, god damn it! Don't spend time persuading them. You can lead a horse to the water, but you can't make it take a sip no matter how hard you suck its behind.

But if you build an alternative and become successful, the demons will fall and good people will follow you on the journey toward a better future.

The Piss Ant

Chinese water torture is the torture of monotony. The victim is hit by drops falling at brief intervals on the same spot. After a while, the sound and the pain becomes unbearable.

This subtle art is the home turf of the Piss Ant, who will patiently and aggressively attack, so that, when you explode, it can step back and viciously proclaim, "Wow, I never saw a more thin-skinned and overly sensitive creature. Relax already!"

The Piss Ant is the type that really should know better (which is why they're not stupid, but evil) and who are scary beasts because they make you look like a self-made disaster. Luckily, the consequences are rarely very severe. Yes, you might make a fool of yourself on their account, but hey, join the club.

We only laugh at you, because we know the feeling. We've also been laughed at by a seriously annoying homunculus, who in all his shady sombreness squinted zit – zit – zit – zit, while we grew more and more peppery and angry.

The Piss Ant may be an authority, like a school teacher or a really horrible boss. An older American women's rights champion told us about an experience she had had with a Piss Ant.

As a young woman in college, she had a teacher, who behaved demeaning and condescending toward women. He consequently gave all of his female students lower grades than their male counterparts. So one day, all the girls switched papers with the boys and the entire class exposed the vicious behavior of the teacher. Like she said, "Never deny people the consequences of their own inappropriate actions."

The utmost supreme defence against the Piss Ant is therefore 'verbal aikido,' a martial art form, which teaches you to be quick and cheeky and use the opponents own arguments against themselves. You adjust to the intention of the opponent and then guide them in a more appropriate direction, in which neither the aggressor nor the offender is hurt. In this way, you exemplify another way of living together, where we can uphold our own boundaries without offending others.

In the movie called 'The Pursuit of Happiness,' Will Smith plays Chris Gardner, a homeless man, who's on his way to the job interview of his life. if he doesn't get the job, his life as a homeless continues. If, on the other hand, he lands the offer, he'll be well on his way toward 'the American Dream.' But before the interview, everything has gone wrong. And a potential Piss Ant situation is looming, when the boss looks at Chris and asks, "What would you say if a guy walked in for an interview without a shirt on, and I hired him? What would you say?" And then Chris answers, "… He must have had on some really nice pants."

Verbal aikido doesn't always work though, and if things are already boiling, you have our permission to step on it and let out some steam. Just drive yourself over the edge. Knock down the Piss Ant, be furiously mad and get it out of your system. And then breathe. The worst thing is to go home embittered and repressed. So if things have already gone completely wrong, you might as well let it all out. The advantage of going the whole hog is:

- It's good for your body.
- It's hard not to laugh at the end.
- It will affect those who deserve it and not your family, friends or the carpark attendant.
- Do it on TV and you'll go viral and gain world fame over night.

All demons upgrade at some point and so the Piss Ant is also hiding in your cell phone and on your computer, where it turns on notifications and sign up for newsletters. It just loves to disturb you by presenting you with a whole lot of nothings and trivialities, so that it can train your autopilot to respond to the ding-ding-dings and swoosh sounds without you noticing. The Piss Ant wins when you have spent the whole day fiddling with unimportant tasks instead of checking off a few important tasks on your list – which will be the source of irritation when you go to bed at night. Turn off the fiddling and take your life and your energy back. Immerse yourself in the important stuff and set yourself free.

The Procrastinator

The motto of the Procrastinator is: 'You must indulge before you can revel.' This demon is king of pleasure and coziness and has one mission in life, which is to lure you into an eternal cocoon condition, where you'll never really develop. All that is painful, difficult, hard, smells and hurts must be wrong.

But note the difference between 'difficult' and 'hard.' 'Difficult' is when you don't have a clue as to what to do (and by the way, you'll get the tools for this in Chapter 10 where we talk about skills and techniques).

'Hard' is when you don't really bother.

To believe that you can go through life without experiencing hardship is a delusion. Hard is not wrong. It just is what it is. No matter how good, lovely and talented you are, there will always be a door frame to bump into, someone you love will be sick or die, and tribalistic idiots will steal your ideas, your energy and your lunch box. Bummer! You've definitely earned yet another weekend of jumping into your pj's, ordering take away and reloading with Netflix and games for the next 2, 6, 38 hours.

But the fact is that the only reason the world is a nice place is because good people get out of bed every day and make good deeds, even though they don't bother. In principle, life is not fair and it never was. Good people are making the world great with the purpose of giving everyone an opportunity to create a good life. And the majority does so humbly without expecting a medal in return. Think about our forefathers who lived through some crazy shit for our sake. What would they think if they saw us today? "Okay, so y'all grew kind a chubby and tired, huh?"

If we take the exemplary game changer from the tutorial, we can all agree that in the future we shouldn't work 'more,' we should work 'better.' Which sounds great! But what if we equate:

Work more: do what you normally do, what you're used to doing and what feels comfortable.

Work better: Renew yourself, shake up old patterns, make annoying changes.

Now, that's harder.

Mark our words: You can't be a game changer, futurist, and a real, living human being creating amazing and beautiful things for you and everyone else and also live a comfortable life all the time. It's not gonna f*cking happen. Comfort must die.

The Procrastinator usually wants to teddy-cuddle when your batteries are running low. The best you can do is to be mindful about your energy resources and stay on top of your game. Better be rich and in physical great shape than poor and sick. The Game of the Future doesn't distinguish between rich and poor, high or low energy, though. All good things in life, as well as the bad, are interconnected. If you wake up and feel energized, you'll brush your teeth, eat healthier, exercise more, you'll be happier at work, pay more attention to opportunities, and be more helpful. If, on the other hand, you get fired and it's raining, your bike has a flat tire and your partner is cranky, it's easy to team up with the Procrastinator and make yourself comfortable with a bowl of chocolate chip cookies on the couch. There you are, all alone as everyone leaves you, and when you die, your cat will eat you.

Low energy levels breed low energy levels, Your job is to be able to reboot and kickstart yourself, if you're headed into a negative spiral. For obviously, being a 'Comfy Connie' is allowed every now and then. But know that the Procrastinator is the demon you can actually train. Make time for some 'hygge' and indulge. Do it without feeling bad.

Enjoy and be happy! The Procrastinator is like a leech. You might think it's doing you good for a little while, but if it's stuck to your leg for too long, it'll suck all the energy out of you, so you end up all tired and lazy.

So many great ideas have been lost on account of a futurist tripping over his or her Procrastinator and taking a soft fall into the couch.

It takes energy to generate energy. Life can feel heavy at times, yes. Like pushing a heavy-duty lorry on a rainy day. When it's rolling, it's easy, but when the road is uphill, it's hard. Very hard. But when you keep focusing on the task ahead of you and invest your energy in an optimum manner, you'll have plenty of time for couch living.

Moderation in all things, and when the Procrastinator tempts you to divert from the road, remind yourself of what is at stake.

The Eraser

This demon is directly related to your autopilot and is capable of resetting your brain in the morning, so you forget your vision, your life's calling and all your good intentions. Worst of all, you may even forgot that you forgot! Have you ever discovered a piece of paper in your drawer that had amazing ideas and insights written on it, and then you realize you wrote it? Yup, that's the Eraser at work.

Forgetting is a good thing, though. You need to sort and filter things in order to function. And you do have a lot of dead weight, knowledge and memories you don't need to carry around. If you don't clear out, your RAM will soon be overloaded and so you won't have the energy to do the work you need to do.

It's awful when the Eraser has erased too much. There's a reason why rituals, habits, discipline and religion took up a lot of space throughout time, for our forefathers also suffered under the smudged fingerprints of the Eraser.

When you invest in cultivating new habits, you hack the autopilot and know very well that change doesn't come overnight. If you keep to it and take a disciplined approach, you'll do great. If you don't, you'll need something to believe in, a calling or a higher purpose, something to motivate you and a community that has your back. Rules, routines and great buddies, who can push and cheer you on when you need it, and create new and great habits together.

Routines, rituals and discipline are some of the strategies you can use to defeat the demons, which is one of the many purposes of religion. An atheist would say that religion is just a set of rules and discipline in a mythical framework. The good story and the higher meaning

educate and increase your consciousness, as they dictate practicing
kindness toward your family and that you're not allowed to steal or
fuck whomever you like. You made a promise – and so we'll see you
next Sunday, when we repeat the pledge you made, so you don't forget.

Much can be said about the festive season, but in the end it's a good
thing for us to meet and sit around the table and make an effort to act
with kindness toward each other, bring presents and think about the
value of gratitude and forgiveness.

You're not stupid for forgetting. In the book, 'The Checklist
Manifesto,' the surgeon Atul Gawande describes how much is at
stake if flight attendants, doctors, nurses and construction workers
fuck up, if they don't constantly and every single time they perform a
procedure stick to their checklists.

You can use the Eraser to your advantage, for this demon is in the
game to cheat you. If you forget, and also forget that you forgot, then
why not forget the things you know you don't need?

There are examples of how dementia (although it's a truly horrible
disease) can in fact bring peace to families, because the person
suffering from memory loss simple can't remember the bitterness or
the conflict anymore. Your brain remembers the things you remind
yourself of and the stories you keep telling yourself. Remind yourself
of what's important. Weed out what you no longer need and cultivate
the things you want to see grow. Create your own ritual, your own
magical universe.

Write down your vision on the home screen of your smartphone or the
desktop on your computer, keep an amulet in your pocket and spend
five minutes writing the same over and over again in your notebook
every day. Put up a letter to yourself on the inside of the door to the
bathroom and use music, smells, sounds and tastes to activate your
memory.

Complex Rex

Complex Rex is one of the most fearsome and formidable opponents in the game. But have no fear, for this demon is (like they say in Texas) 'all hat and no cattle,' With his big head and short arms, he thunders toward you like an overly well-read and pompous dinosaur from the age of Tribal. Complex Rex just loves to overcomplicate stuff and make things more intricate than they actually are. He will stand over you like a dark shadow and say things like, "My dear, I don't think you understand just how complicated this is. When you've been here as long as I have, you will see that it's not that simple." Impeding your process before you've actually started and making you feel like a naive nonentity, who doesn't have a proper education or shoulders wide enough to carry the load, is the mission of this demon.

Education and knowledge are great things in the world, and we must respect history and all that. Unfortunately, when people invoke respect for history, it's usually not history (what actually happened) that they talk about. They refer to their own history and they want to call special attention to their vantage point, where everything begins and all identity springs from, and let's all sing the same canonical song.

You're not a bad person if you don't know the list of kings and queens by heart, and yes, you are allowed to create amazing things even though you can't remember what the Battle of Waterloo was all about. And no, that online course or this skills upgrade is not going to make a difference what so ever if you don't allow (or prepare) for magic in the front seat.

Complex Rex has a habit of pulling the plug on all action, making people waste time by reducing risks and overanalyzing everything that can co wrong. If we did the same before we decided to get pregnant, humanity would be extinct with the next generation.

When you're in the process of creating yourself and designing solutions which have never been seen before, it is a huge advantage not knowing everything beforehand. This will make room for the surprises and coincidences inherent in all innovation and inventive thinking.

So many organizations forget this part. And then they completely lose sight of radical change.

Personally, we have fought our share of Complex Rexes at middle manager level, and every single time, it is the same story all over again. So much time and effort is spent on generating a small effect. A few years back, we were in the ring boxing a huge, Danish supermarket chain and after a generous amount of research, infographics, workshops and us playing around with different futures and trends, this supermarket chain finally decided only to move the jam and the peanut butter and place them by the toast bread section. A mind-blowing move in their optics. "Jam and peanut butter together, are you crazy!? The jam manager would then have to coordinate with the toast bread manager, and they hate the peanut butter girl!"

Complex Rex will laugh all the way back to the cave wondering how little it actually takes to make things seem so intricate and confusing adding a little apathy on top. He'll use words like 'discourse' and 'context' to scare people off, or he'll say things like, "I have this rule and it lasts forever! For this is how it is and always was."

Complex Rex just loooooves stupid rules.

The British street urchin chef (and game changer), Jamie Oliver, visited a school in the USA, where the kids had the saddest and most slimy food for lunch. He tried to introduce vegetables to the menu, but he was up against some tough cookies. The kitchen chef gave him a tired look and said, "French fries are vegetables?" To which Jamie answered, "Well, yeah-naaa," and she took out a pen to check off the field, 'School children must eat vegetables every day:' Check!

Cut to Jamie sitting outside the building in tears: "Can't they see I'm just here to help? They're pushing an entire generation of school kids over the edge!"

Kill Your Darling Demons

Now you know the demons. Use this knowledge to build your defence, so you can avoid and ignore them and minimize the time, energy and thinking power you spend on them.

Note also that demons tend to triangulate, meaning they join forces in groups of three to surround and nag at you. So keep an eye out for the top three demons praying on you.

Know that the demons get their energy from making you suffer.

You can't avoid pain and grief. Grief is usually an immediate response, whereas suffering typically is chronic. Grief is when something factual hits you right in the face. Suffering is your response to the grief, the story you tell yourself. Notice how you can actually be relieved of suffering by applying a different meaning to it. Just because you get a parking ticket, you don't have to hand over your cheerfulness. Accept the grief and the pain. Say, "Fuck, fuck, fuck!" and "well, well." Let it out of your system and then move on in the game.

Think your own thoughts and decide your mood yourself.

Spend your energy, your money and your surplus on important things.

Fight for your beliefs.

Stand up and keep standing up!

And remember, it's often more important to be fun than smart.

Piss Off Island

Everyone has an island, which is entirely their own. It has dolphins and palm trees and a cocktail bar and all the things that make you happy. You can always withdraw to this island, where you'll be protected. Only the things you let happen are allowed to happen.

A bit further out in the sea, about half a mile from your island, is another island. It's called the 'Piss Off Island' and there's a ferry back and forth between them every day. If someone pisses on your island, put them on that ferry until they've learned how to behave.

Level 6
CONQUER YOUR VANTAGE POINT

WHO DOES THE WORLD NEED YOU TO BE?

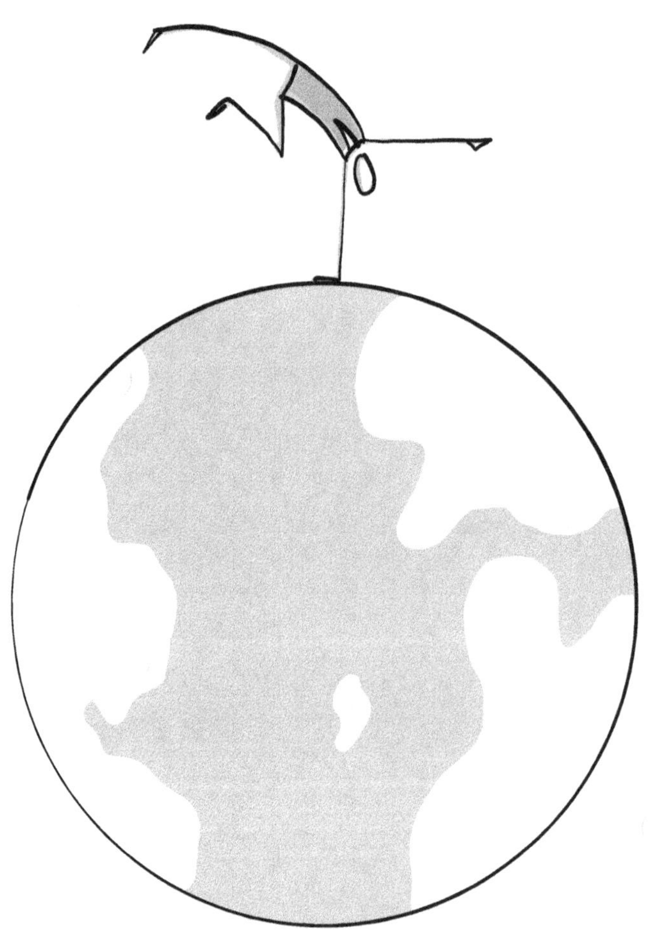

Chapter 9
CONQUER YOUR VANTAGE POINT

For thousands of years, the Oracle of Delphi was the center of the world. People (high and low) traveled here to get answers and insights about the future. Above the gate to the temple forecourt, the maxim "Know thyself" was inscribed, for only those who sincerely sought and spent the journey looking inward would understand the message. No prospect without insight. Actually, the full sentence reads, "Know thyself and you shall know the universe and the gods." Well, hello!

The vantage point is where you currently are in your life. Without a starting point, you can't place yourself in relation to the future. The trends that are important for education are not necessarily as important for travel agencies, the military or other industries and vice versa. When you work with the future, it's essential to determine, examine and question your vantage point.

A vantage point is also a container of identity. Old military strategies use this as the central most important position, be it a ridge, a fort, a strategic location, that many soldiers throughout time have given their lives for conquering. This point holds the power and advantage on the battle field of the entire army.

Whether you want to or not, you are standing on your own ridge. You don't just give that up, for that would meaning exposing who

you are and how you view the world. This is where your future
meets the present and the past. So, if life seems like a mess to you, if
you're confused about the future, or if everything seems sinister and
annoying, it's a sign that you need to update your vantage point.

Using trends is the most optimal tool to transform your vantage
point. When you look and behold the future, you should ask yourself,
"Should I defend my vantage point? Is this still right for me? Or do I
need to abandon it and start searching for another peak in my life?

It's also convenient to ask yourself, "Who am I in the world? Who
do I want to be? And what does the world need me to be?" Feel free
to make up more questions that will guide you to your next vantage
point.

Out of Sync

History is full of people, who looked to the future, spotted the right
trends, but didn't do anything about them. It happens all the time,
make peace with it. You can't choose what trends are most important
to you and make full use of them, if your vantage point is out sync.
Neither can your audience.

CASE: The Cars of the Future And New Status Symbols
In our time, we've worked on the future together with some of the
big car manufacturers and importers in the world. And when we ask
them what their game changer is, they all currently reply, "Electric
and self-driving cars." The fact that a lot of manufacturers still don't
develop this type of vehicle, in spite of this answer, is according to
themselves not because they can't afford it or because they don't have
the opportunity or are not able to spot the same trends as Elon Musk,
the man behind Tesla cars, or that they don't think it's vital for the
future. So, why aren't they doing anything about it?

A guy like Elon Musk is a visionary, because he has found his vantage
point. He has two strategies:

- Saving the planet with electric cars (and change the rules of the game).
- If saving the planet doesn't succeed, then we're moving to Mars.

The traditional car industry maintains a vantage point from before the last financial crisis. They're still overly excited when the cup holder slides back into the chassis with a neat click sound. And they still aim for the market segment they know the best, C-level drivers.

The Tesla is a great bridge to the future. It signals far more virility than the Ellert and it's the car your kids want to drive. We actually know a CEO, who had to get rid of his sledge of a gasoline car, because the kids pretended not to know him when he drove in it.

If you have a hard time letting go of your vantage point, because it's too painful to create a new vantage point, the game ends here. Instead of moving up in levels, in time, you'll be reduced to an 'old gamer,' a walk-on extra, a villain or an obstacle for other players in the game. Particularly, if you're a white middle-aged man in an attractive job with a pale network and a colorless resume – we're looking at you.

Interestingly, there's an indication that those who are most likely to win the Game of the Future in the centuries to come are the ones with a shitty vantage point. It could be the men and women in Africa, for instance, as they have far less to lose than people in the western world, who have so much shit that they're practically drowning. Other runner-ups are young people who can't get a foothold in the Monopoly-inspired labor market, people without a proper retirement plan, or those who long to reinvent themselves or simply want to rebel against the system.

High Society And Visions Without Windows

We were once invited to give a brief and provocative presentation about the future of education and the labor market to some of the most distinguished and powerful institutions in Denmark. The event was held in a basement without windows two stories below ground level. Everyone seemed cranky and the room was cold. Several VIPs complained loudly that the seat they had been given was too far away from the stage compared to their self-imposed importance in the industry. In short: the atmosphere was depressing. There was a lot of Mind and Body, but not a whole lot of Soul.

We presented three hard trends, which in our estimate could (and still can) change society in a more radical direction – for the better – within the next ten years:

- **The long life - The good life**: Success is no longer to live a long life. We want a better life and make heavy demands on what a better life means. Also, the difference between those who are doing well and those who suffer will be bigger. If we don't do anything about it, the rich will be healthier and the poor will be more sick.

- **Retirement - Rest of my life:** Or, "from retirement to pretirement." A global trend, where the young generations learn and teach themselves to save up enough money to be financially independent early in life. This means that they can flex in and out of the work force their whole life through. They'll be able to take a break for a few years, for instance when they start a family, or when they grow tired of it all and want a change of scenery career-wise. We can work for as long as we like and are able to, but we'll have far more freedom and flexibility.

- **Education - Training:** School is never out. We'll see new ways of learning that are fun and interactive. Not just in educational institutions, but in ways that can be customized to our personal learning preferences, time schedule and mood. The more skilled and talented we become, the more we can earn and create and the faster we can come home and do something else.

At this event, we felt like we were talking to a big, black hole. Like explaining color to the color-blind. There was no curiosity and no one felt like saying, "Well, that's interesting." In the following debate, all panelists quickly agreed that none of our trends were likely to happen, so they might as well carry on and do business as usual. It was clear

as day that the futurists were really annoying and that everyone just
wanted us to leave.

So, we did!

We still predict, however, that we need to shake things up a bit and
look beyond wages, time and conditions of employment to solve
the problems we see with regard to stress, loneliness, productivity,
supplementary training, the ageing society, polarization, diversity, etc.
The list goes on. The problems arose in Tribal and can only be solved
(for the better) in Planetary. But as long as the people in charge don't
let go of their old vantage point, it will not happen. And yes, it is hard.
It's downright anxiety-provoking. But what if employees would rather
be released than retained?

Where do we find more magic and more irritation? In defending the
past or in creating the future?

Discover Your Principles
(Hint: They Already Discovered You)

If your vantage point still isn't clear as day to you, and if you feel the
future calling, there's help to be found in your 'defining principles.'

Your principles are that part of you which you can't compromise
with without feeling that you're selling out. A principle for a nurse,
for instance, is 'care.' If a nurse doesn't experience magic moments in
taking care of other people, he or she needs to find another job.

A report on the healthcare system documented that nurses in
particular are prone to experience stress in relation to contact with
patients, to which end the very same report recommended a reduction
in the time spent between nurses and patients.

If we work from a different starting point, we'll find that contact
with patients and care are defining principles and that if nurses are

coming down with stress, we have to give them better opportunities for providing more (and better) care for their patients.

PRINCIPLES ARE STRONG INDIVIDUALLY, BUT PUT TOGETHER THEY IGNITE PURE MAGIC.

PRINCIPLES WEEP WHEN WE COMPARE THEM.

PRINCIPLES ARE NOT THE SAME AS VALUES.

Values are something you strive for, a declaration of intent. Values are also elastic, which means that you can stretch or tighten them depending on the circumstances.

Principles, on the other hand, define and restrict you. You can't choose your principles yourself, for they have already chosen you. They are already an intrinsic part of the fabric that is you, and so you can't ignore or get rid of them. They shape your identity, so let them guide you and find your strength in them. Use them as an excuse for bad behavior and they will feel inflexible and like they're weighing you down. If you ignore them, you'll feel that you're selling out. And if you don't live by them, it will feel like your energy is being sucked out of you. In time, you'll come down with stress, die slowly on the inside, and that flame of passion that gets you out of bed every morning will simply burn out.

Principles are not an either or, they are a matter of yes and no. Your principles amplify each other and make you flourish and grow.

Notice especially two things in your every day life.

Dilemmas will put your principles to the test. Either, when they're measured up against each other, against values or the expectations of others.

IT And the Status of The White Man

The Dutchman, Guido van Rossum, is one of the most influential programmers we know of. He rarely gives interviews, but when he does, he shoots out very bold and distinct statements. "The last thing I want to do," he said in 2019, "is to be a mentor for other white men."

KAPOW! Like when Batman gave the bad guys a good beating in the old TV-show. The rules of the game in programming have become planetary, and Guido knows this. In the old days, it used to be a boys' class, and they would sit around all day in their parents' garage and geek out. Today, IT is open source, global, 24/7, diverse and multicultural. The white man is no longer automatically an epic player, which means that the person Guido van Rossum needs to be in the world, the vantage point he must conquer, no longer is the bad-ass king among equals. Instead, he is going to build the bridge and be the kind facilitator that encourages very different people to work better together.

Guido van Rossum saw how IT-projects succeed, when people commit over longer periods of time and work in an atmosphere, where it's safe to share e-mail addresses, ideas and provide constructive feedback to colleagues you've never actually met in person. White men are the bullies here. They are too sure of themselves and have got nothing to show for it. Women and minorities are being completely run over.

According to Guido, the different attitudes toward women and men in the programmer community are fundamentally a problem that society to solve. And we have to solve it from the bottom up. "I've always felt that feminism was right and that we have to change society in every respect," he said in the same interview.

In the meantime, Guido van Rossum feels responsible for changing the rules of the game in areas where he can influence them. Consequently, he only mentors women and underrepresented minorities. "White guys, forget about it," he says, "they are not the ones who need it the most. Men needs a lesson in their own bias. Some guys are super defensive and annoyed, but they just don't know better. So, this is in fact also to their advantage."

Stress is another indicator. You come down with stress, among other things, when you compromise with you principles, when you feel that you're selling out.

In order to see how it works, we'll borrow an example from biochemistry and the German biochemist and game changer, Justus von Liebig.

In the 19th century, Justus von Liebig invented the stock cube, superphosphate, infant formula and baking powder. He found his passion (and magic moments) in the process of figuring out how farmers and housewives could optimize the remedies they had at their disposal.

His best friend's little girl died of cholera. This was a loss that took a toll on Justus. But his friend's daughter wasn't the only one who died. In the 19th century, it was completely normal for a baby who had lost its mother to die if a wet nurse wasn't available.

These deaths made such an impression on von Liebig that his new vantage point become how to nourish and feed the world: to release the potential of living organisms (particularly in agriculture) and support the sick, starved and poor and help them improve their quality of life.

The discovery you need in order to find and define your principles is called Liebig's Law of the Minimum.

Liebig's Law states that the growth of a plant always depends on the scarcest principle that determines the output of growth, meaning that the scarcest resource controls and restricts the growth the most. For example, in order for a plant to grow and unfold its potential, it needs a few, but very essential ingredients every day: water, sunlight, nutrients, something to grow in, CO_2, and love.

All plants depend on these few factors to grow, but they don't need
them in the same amounts. A hot field with lots of sunlight and rain is
not the most optimal place to grow a mushroom, for instance, whereas
a pineapple would thrive in this environment. In return, the pineapple
will not benefit from the dimmed lighting, temperature and humidity
of a basement in the same way as the mushroom. The width of the
staves in the barrel graphic shows how much the plant needs. Some
plants, like for instance a cactus, need almost no love (understood
as the conditions and the kindness provided by the surroundings),
whereas basils and strawberries are serious prima donnas.

When all factors, or principles, are present, it's the height of the stave
that limits the growth of the plant. If there's not enough sunlight,
it won't do any good to pour more water and add another nutrient.
When the plant then gets the sunlight, it will grow to the next level,
which is defined by the next limiting factor, which could be the growth
media. If the soil is wrong or if there's not enough room, the plant will
no longer thrive.

A great farmer is aware of this principle, and he'll make daily assessments as to what needs his plants have. If it rains, there's no need for added fertilizer. If the sun is shining, he can add more nutrient. It's never a case of either or, it's always a question of yes and no.

It's important to understand that the principles of the plant only apply up to a certain level. If a plant gets too much water, it'll drown. If it gets too much sunlight or fertilizer, it will die.

When we transfer this model to other complex systems, everything becomes so much easier. Some people thrive inside office buildings, while others need fresh air and natural settings. Some people need praise and acknowledgement on a daily basis in order to function, while others will vomit if they get too much. Some people carry a childhood trauma of broken homemade pottery and consequently, they need stronger hoops around their barrel, people to take extra good care of them. If they get that, they'll flourish just as nicely as the next person.

Years ago, before the age of the iPad, an Indian professor conducted an experiment of placing a computer in a wall in an Indian village. The result was a steep and rising learning curve among the local children. This idea spread to the rest of the world, for if technology was able to release so much potential in an Indian village, schools all over the world ought to have an iPad or a computer for every kids in class. But did it have the same effect? No! For in India, technological access to knowledge was a delimiting factor. In the western world, the delimiting factors are different – motivation, teacher contact, etc.

Find Your Principles And Conquer Your Vantage Point

You can use this model to find and define your principles. What does it take for you to thrive in your everyday life? When are you growing, flourishing and thriving?

Identify at least three and maximum six principles. Because the principles define who you are, people should be able to recognize you in them. We, your authors, have creativity as a defining principle, we don't thrive with routines, but have an amazing time in stressful situations like presenting the future to a crowd of 2,000 people. If we were not allowed to publish and present our ideas and knowledge, if no one was at the receiving end of our stories, we would be sure to wither and die. At home, Anne's husband used to hold a distinguished position as C-level manager at the global container logistics company, A.P. Moller – Maersk. But he reached a point in his life, where he was slowly languishing from a poor indoor climate. So he quit his job and is now thriving again, because his everyday life is filled with kids, the splendid outdoors, forests, canoeing and carpentry. It's not unusual to realize halfway in your life that your biggest magic moments come out of cutting something out of wood. Henrik is married to a singer, who loves to create stuff with her hands, be it cake, jewellery, and facilitating a better life for patients in rehabilitation therapy.

You'll know your principles, when you can say, "This is me in a nut shell," or, "I feel at home on this shelf." Imagine a world where school is all about individual learning according to the kids' defining principles, helping the seeds to grow on their own terms? In this way, children would be enabled to spend their lives cultivating the things they were magically born to be.

Inspiration for Your Principles

Use this list as inspiration and draw up your own version of
Liebig's model. How tall and how wide should it be? What
is your limiting factor at this point? Just begin and exchange
your principles as you become more aware of who you
really are. In the end, you'll have a list of three to six words.
The process can take months, even years, which is perfectly
okay.

- Freedom
- Flexibility
- Acknowledgement
- Balance
- Challenges
- Independence
- Sports
- Equality
- Innovation
- Leadership
- Sustainability
- Integrity
- Spontaneity
- Learning
- Development
- Experimentation
- Community
- Variation
- Growth
- Authenticity
- Diversity
- Professionalism
- Co-creation
- Security
- Charity
- Team work

- Prestige
- Fun
- Higher meaning
- Pride
- Surprices
- Peace
- Problem solving
- Kindness
- Rebellious
- Frontline fighter
- Adrenalin
- Dedication
- Dignity
- Orderliness
- Curiosity
- Love
- Sex
- Family
- Nearness
- Traveling
- Experiences
- Influence

When you've identified your principles and if you 'tend to your plant' every day, it doesn't mean everything in your life will be 100% woohooo amazing from now on. You'll actually just be neutral. Your lowest point will be high, and you'll not be easily knocked out. From this point you'll be able to think visionary thoughts and create what you and the rest of the world need. And you'll be able to turn down opportunities and say a loud and confident 'yes' to the many new possible directions life can take you.

You've found the road home to yourself.

Tourist or Futurist?

You can go sightseeing and be a modern Dr. Livingstone hunting for new discoveries. If you ever feel stressed out or under pressure in the Game of the Future, you can seek sanctuary in the safety zone called 'the Tourist.'

A tourist is traveling and sightseeing. As a tourist, you don't have to do anything and nobody needs to notice you're there. The tourist is curious by nature and keeps and open mind, but s/he's also neutral and can freely wander around and navigate the Game of the Future.

The only thing you have to master in order to go from Tribal to Tourist is taking a break. Yes, take a break. Step back for a while and take a look at the greater picture without responding. Just observe. As a tourist, you must listen to your MBS. If you think, "We usually…" or "my dreams can't come true…" your future sense must call for a full stop.

Remember that everything that is urgent is yelling, while everything that is important is whispering. And your future sense in the tourist mode does just that: observes and whispers very quietly in your ear what you really need to hear in order to gain insight, which you often find a pain in the neck and therefore ignore.

All you have to do is to say: "Well, Well."

You can always panic later.

Later is always the best time to panic.

The Exponential Tourist

Exponentiality is a trend that a lot of futurists believe will dominate the future. 'Exponential' refers to a development that is constantly doubled instead of running a linear course. It's often communicated as something dangerous. For example in this metaphor visualizing exponential growth:

You're sitting in a football stadium on the highest seat with the best overview. The time is 1pm. This particular stadium is completely waterproof. From above, a pipette starts to drip water on your stadium. First one drop, then two, then four, etc. Every minute the number of drops is doubled. How long does it take before you must get up from your seat and leave the stadium so as not to drown?

Is it hours, days, weeks months?

The first drop of water lands right in the middle of the field at 1pm. The next two at 1:01pm … The answer is that the stadium will be filled with water at 1:49pm.

It takes less that 50 minutes to fill an entire football stadium with water, when the drops fall exponentially. But it doesn't stop here, for at what time do you think the stadium is still 93% empty?

Take a guess.

The answer is at 1:45pm. So you're basically looking at a puddle for 45 minutes and within the last four minutes things move fast. Really fast.

And then you drown.

We've heard this story so many times presented on a stage in front of an audience, and every time we can sense how their stomaches ache, which is also why people buy the premise of 'exponential organizations' that are 'hyper agile' which again require 'adaptable' employees.

But let's wonder together: Who the hell sits in a waterproof stadium and wait for the water level to rise? And why do stories like this always talk to us like we're a bunch of passive extras? And, if technology do speed up routines and processes exponentially, could you imagine that people then wouldn't have to worry about processes and routines, but

instead would focus their energy on thoughtfulness and originality instead? And that we need to be really good at making 360 degree decisions and not just run faster and faster?
Human beings can easily take part in an exponential development. We do it every day, actually. Have you ever tried having a messy house and just as you're about to give up, it's like everything falls into place just in time? This is also exponentiality. Another constructive image is puzzle games. If we were to piece together a puzzle of, say, 5,000 pieces, we'd go about with a glass of red wine and some 'hygge.' We'd turn the pieces one by one, find and define the edges first and begin mapping it out the framework together. In the beginning, it's a real mess, but all of a sudden we see how the pieces fall into place. Hey, here's a cloud, look, isn't that a part of the horse? Faster and faster, and eventually, the final pieces are placed at the speed of light. Exponential speed.

And we're not drowning, thank goodness. And, what's more important, nobody's losing. The winner might be the person, who gets to place the final piece, but the biggest success is that we had fun together. Everybody wins, no one looses.

So, don't let yourself be carried away anymore, you're always allowed to take a break.

A tourist is neutral. The calm center in the eye of the hurricane, where there's peace and quiet in just listening and observing.

When you meet the world with a neutral, open and curious "well, well," the next step is to seek out the annoying, dangerous, exciting, fun and enriching stuff in life.

And then you become a futurist. A phew-tourist.

There are lots of different ways to be a futurist and it's about time you find your own.

Channel the Powers of the Seven Futurists

Futurists can be divided into seven archetypes, who has their own strengths and weaknesses.

At all times, kings, military commanders, leaders and ordinary people have visited wise men and women to have a look into the unknown, mysterious future.

These futurists are categorized in seven archetypes. You don't have to settle on just one type. Experiment so you learn what style suits you better and use that to lift up your audience.

If you need to argue in front of a tech-savvy audience, you can use the methods of scientific futurists. If your audience is a group of creatives, you can tap into the work of the more artistic and intuitive futurists. If you're not certain, then try and channel the self-confidence of the oracle, the guru or the ability of the cartographer to detect patterns and make sense of chaos. If you need inspiration for taking action, then check out the surfer or the explorer.

THE ORACLE

"Whether you think you can do it or not, you're right."

Description
The oracle is the ancient and historical go-to person, when it comes to foresight. The oracle has an almost uncanny ability to see into the future. It was assumed to be an instrument of insightful divinity and so the audience were to bring gifts in order to receive the wise words.

Characteristics
Convincing, charismatic, inspiring, manipulative, and a little crazy.

Argumentation
Mysterious, cryptic, and quirky. Lots of room for interpretation and gut feeling.

Trend spotting
Based on intuition, emotions and divine inspiration. And drugs.

Modern version
Oracles might not be able to explain the reason why they see a trend and they don't really care. They want to read books, articles and carry out their research, but in reality, they're intuitive, emotional beings, who sense and experience the world with every fiber of their being.

As an oracle, you'll 'feel an increasing tendency' and argue through storytelling and narratives that are open to interpretation.

Positive attributes
Sees the amazing future before anyone else using intuition only.

Negative attributes
Too vague or cryptic. Easily misunderstood. No interaction with the audience.

FAMOUS ORACLES

Pythia
Also known as the Oracle of Delphi, the far most famous and respected oracle in the ancient Greco-Roman world. Pythia was considered the center of the world, and for more than a thousand years, some of the most important characters of history felt compelled to visit the temple before making important decisions. Above the gate to the temple was an inscription, "Know thyself," as it was considered a precondition for being able to interpret the words of the oracle.

Nostradamus
A French astrologer, physician and famous seer, widely known for his book, 'Les Prophéties,' a collection of 942 poems predicting future events. The book was published in 1555 and hasn't been out of print since. His arguments in the book are vague and ambiguous, but they're written in a way that attracts a wide audience.

THE PROPHET

"Revealing the truth is like striking a match, it may bring light or it may set your world on fire."

Description
The scientific and methodologically oriented trend spotter. Prophets are distinguished by their love for data collection, statistic overviews and forecasts. They can identify the future like no others. They are amazingly talented at 'proving their claims' and building strong evidence around their trends and arguments.

Characteristics
Likes being right about the future. Precise. Correct. Might seem like s/he is a little possessed.

Argumentation
High on science and specific case studies. Usually highlights one important trend, message or world view.

Trend spotting
Based on facts, data, cases and real life examples.

Modern version
A prophet extracts insight from a solid foundation or a belief. For some, it's a religion or a mystic world view. For others, it's science, a

discipline or a subject area. Prophets often reach a conclusion, a 'truth' or an insight, which they feel compelled to share with the world.

Positive attributes
Very clear viewpoints. Sees the undeniable future. Creates a sense of urgency.

Negative attributes
Application range is too small. Boring. Stigmatized as a fool. Stubborn and uncompromising.

Famous prophets

Edmund Halley
British astronomer, geophysicist, mathematician, meteorologist, and physicist. He employed the laws of nature to calculate the periodicity of comets and was ridiculed by his co-researchers, but gained fame and praise, when a comet (as predicted) showed up on the night sky. In 1758, at its predicted return, it was named after him, which he unfortunately didn't live long enough to see.

Muhammed
The founder of Islam. A prophet sent to confirm the monotheistic teachings as previously lectured by Adam, Abraham, Moses and Jesus. Muhammad united Arabia in one single Muslim policy. In his later years, he would hide in a cave, where Gabriel the archangel would visit to bring revelations from God.

Nikola Tesla
A Serbian-American inventor, electrical engineer, mechanical engineer and futurist, best known for his contribution to the design of the modern system of alternating current. Tesla also invented wireless recharging, the radio and predicted the smartphone, wifi, the autopilot and self-driving vehicles.

THE GURU

"If you change your mind, you change the world."

Description
Gurus are authorities in their fields of expertise. They create change through followers. People might not understand what you're saying, but because you're a guru, they'll believe you because you seem really clever.

Characteristics
Wants to impact and set things in motion. They are driven by a dream or a vision about the future. Dedicated, passionate. May come across as a little too uncontroversial or eccentric.

Argumentation
Grand storytellers, who can connect the hearts and minds of their audience. Loves the abstract and hypothetical stuff.

Trend spotting
A guru uses all sorts of techniques to observe trends and they are amazing at connecting the dots. They use their charisma to make others see.

Modern version
Gurus are often experts and masters of many fields. They typically have a wide intellectual horizon and a deep-felt respect for the artistic as well as the scientific parts of futurology. What they really want is to move the world.

Today, we see them on social media and business platforms or at financial and political gatherings, where they can reach people and decision makers.

Positive attributes

Thousands, no, millions of followers are inspired by the guru's vision and then the world progresses. For instance, Martin Luther King's "I have a dream"-speech.

Negative attributes

Uses charisma to enhance his or her own agenda without substantial facts or responsibility to back it up. For instance, Nathan Thompson and the Flat Earth Society.

Famous gurus

Mahatma Gandhi

An Indian activist and leader of the Indian independence movement fighting against the colonial British rule. Gandhi arranged campaigns based on civil disobedience and led India to independence, which inspired other movements of civil rights and freedom all over the world. Gandhi was a great listener, extremely patient and was also able not just to 'see' the future, but to encourage an entire nation to choose another path.

Steve Jobs

An American business magnate and investor, co-founder of Apple Inc., Pixar and NeXT. Jobs is widely renowned and recognized for his pioneer work revolutionizing the microcomputer in the 1970s and 1980s, together with Apple co-founder Steve Wozniak, whose trend spotting style was that of the cartographer.

Oprah Winfrey

An American celebrity and prominent media star, actress, talkshow host, television producer, author and philanthropist. She promoted and revolutionized the genre of tabloid talk show and broke down a lot of taboos by for instance inviting people from the LGBT-community to appear on mainstream TV.

THE FORTUNE TELLER

"The best work that anyone ever does happens on the edge of the comfort zone, where the stakes are high and you risk making a fool of yourself."

Description
The fortune teller is the first futurist in history to use props: crystal balls, tea leaves, tarot cards and so on. The fortune teller would swing a dead cat by the tail if it could woo and impress the audience. Because, fortune tellers love just that: making their audience excited.

Characteristics
Opportunistic. Full of fun and surprises. Seems like revealing and digging up the future like a mystery. The whole point is to ignite the imagination and make others see what is meaningful for them.

Argumentation
The fortune teller likes to improvise. It's like jazz. Exceed the sheet music, improvise and let your audience feel the rhythm of your story.

Trend spotting
Based on the needs, wishes, dreams of the audience.

Modern version
There's been a tendency to view fortune tellers as a bunch of quacks
and charlatans, but the best of them are actually great entertainers.
They have that spark of magic in their aura and they love accessories.
Modern fortune tellers use games, apps and interactive tools to create
future perspectives.

Positive attributes
The audience is the most important part of the story. Fun, surprising
and very unpredictable.

Negative version
Takes advantage of the needs of the audience. Takes too much
responsibility instead of just letting people find their own way.

Famous fortune tellers

Madame Lenormand
A 19th century French celebrity famous for her use of tarot cards as
a tool for predicting the future. She moved to Paris to set up a salon
and soon became a celebrity with VIP-followers among her customers.
One of them was the Emperor Napoleon and his wife Josephine. After
a few years, Napoleon grew tired of her accuracy, though, especially
when she predicted his divorce before he got a chance to announce it
to Josephine.

John Dee
An Anglo-Welsh mathematician, astronomer, astrologist, occultist,
philosopher and advisor to Queen Elizabeth I. As a collector, Dee had
one of the largest libraries in England and his high standing as teacher
paved the way for the central role he played in the Elizabethan policy.

The combination of his intellectual nature and understanding of the
superstition of his followers made him use crystals balls and other
artefacts to argue for the future.

THE SURFER

"First come, first served."

Description

The impatient trend spotter. The surfer doesn't care how we understand the future. It's all about seizing the trends and see where they might take us. If we spend time trying to understand a trend, it's already too late.

Characteristics

The surfer is a 'first mover.' One who takes a chance. They are impatient and constantly look for new and exciting areas with the promise of the moon.

Argumentation

Short and to the point. They often don't have time to explain and tend to use expressions like 'fear of missing out' or 'the window of opportunity.'

Trend spotting

Based on experience and intuition, and taking chances.

Modern version
We owe surfers our gratitude. They are the members of the tribe, who
saw the future and took action. They were the first to use fire, they
ate the fruit nobody had ever seen before and for better and worse
welcomed strangers to the camp. Today, surfers are more ordinary.
We typically find them in the fashion industry and in the arena of fast
consumer goods and entrepreneurship.

Positive attributes
Identifies important trends. Changes the world by taking action. Gives
others permission to join in.

Negative attributes
Switches between trends so quickly that no real value can come out of
it. Pays no attention what so ever to the consequences of their actions.

Famous surfers

Anna Wintour
A British-American journalist and editor in chief of Vogue Magazine.
Wintour is an important figure in the fashion industry and is well-
acclaimed for her keen trend eye and support to young designers.
Anna Wintour is in fact so good a predicting the future that she creates
waves of her own.

Andrew Carnegie
A Scottish-American industrialist, business magnate and
philanthropist, surfing the waves of development in steel, which led
to the expansion of the American steel industry in the 19th century
construction of sky scrapers, rail roads, etc. Carnegie is thought to be
one of the richest men in history.

THE EXPLORER

"The best way to predict the future is to create it."

Description

The explorer is driven by an ambition to feel and experience the future and not just sitting around talking about it. Your friends see you as brave and bold, but in reality you're a super curious freedom lover. New things are interesting because they are new!

Characteristics

Very adventurous and brave. Sitting in an office all day reflecting on the world is not what futurism is about.

Argumentation

Fascinating and inspirational arguments based on their own experiences and trends from the original sources.

Trend spotting

Travels to collect data and mixes that with their own ambitions and convictions. Trends are delivered with the intention of taking action.

Modern version

By being prepared to take risks in the face of the unknown, explorers have always pushed our boundaries in the search for discovery and fame.

Today, explorers are scientists, podcasters, people in the media industry and role models doing the things most of us dream of doing. They encourage us with a "just do it!"

Positive attributes
Not afraid to push boundaries. Makes it safe for others to follow in their footsteps. Makes an effort. Experiments.

Negative attributes
Gets lost or forgets to come back. Excludes others from all the fun. Loses respect for the everyday.

Famous explorers

Christopher Columbus
An Italian explorer, navigator, and colonial settler. He led the first European expeditions to the Caribbean, Central and South America, which marked the beginning of the permanent European colonization of the Americas. Columbus discovered a sustainable route to America, a continent not yet known to the old world. He died in false belief that he had discovered East Asia and without remorse for all the people who died as a consequence of his colonial venture.

Nellie Bly
An American journalist famous for her record setting tour around in the world in 72 days inspired by Jules Verne's fictive character, Phileas Fogg. She was also renown for working undercover, reporting from the inside of a psychiatric hospital, among other places.

She was a pioneer in her field and introduced a new type of investigating journalism. Bly was also a writer, industrialist, inventor and a charity worker.

THE CARTOGRAPHER

There are three kinds of people: Those, who see. Those, who see when things are presented to them. And those, who don't see at all.

Description
Among trend spotters, the cartographers are the experts of creating an overview. Their super powers are visualizing and making the future convincing. They collect trends to find patterns, not just in the future, but also in the present and the past. They show us how things are connected and interrelated and change paradigms. They develop maps, models, techniques and methods for others to use.

Characteristics
Organized, methodological and always drawing up some new potential pattern, model or overview. Loves to use trends to compose visualizations.

Argumentation
Comparing and matching patterns for an event that didn't happen yet, Sherlock Holmes-style.

Trend spotting
Based on piles of research from every possible source.

Modern version
The cartographer usually accompanied the explorer. They created maps and models that were crucial for decision makers.

Without them, we wouldn't be able to witness things that went down in history. Today, cartographers are writers, journalists, engineers and researchers, many of whom work undercover as they prefer insight rather than spotlight.

Positive attributes
Creates materials that cause paradigms shifts which again change the world. A helper and a collaborative partner.

Negative attributes
Goes into an ultra geeky mode to work on stuff that will never be done.

Famous cartographers

Leornado da Vinci
An Italian polymath, who lived in the Renaissance and whose interests included inventions, map making, drawing, painting, and sculpture as well as the fields of Architecture, Science, Music, Mathematics, Engineering, Literature, Anatomy, Geology, Astronomy, Botany, Creative Writing, and History. Full stop. He pioneered various fields, such as Paleontology, Ichnology and Architecture and is widely recognized as one of the greatest artists in history. He is credited with the invention of the parachute, the helicopter and the battle tank.

Joan Blaeu
Joan Blaeu worked for the Dutch East India Company and produced a large atlas consisting of hundreds of baroque cards, which very accurately depicted the known continents. He broke with a design tradition that dates back to Ptolemy and placed the Earth at the center of the universe.

Florence Nightingale
An English nurse, statistician and founder of modern nursing. She used infographics to convince Queen Victoria to improve the conditions at military hospitals. And she believed that she did the work of God and that God spoke through statistics.

Design Your Own Futurist

By embracing the arts as well as science you'll lift up both knowledge and imagination to a magical level. We've said it before: You can't win the Game of the Future on your own. You need to find your peeps and combine their knowledge with your own in order to make the best use of your archetype.

Where the past only saw a limited amount of futurists on a global scale, this coming century will see a rise in the number of people, who in very different ways work with the future, a greater diversity in the types and hybrids of futurists.

The connection between the qualitative and quantitative future will prepare the ground for a variety of new futurists, including you and your approach. The quantitative future is controlled by all the information that machines can provide, data and images, and in such huge quantities that we'll be able to predict microlevels of the future. The qualitative future, on the other hand, is guided by behavior, emotions and intuition.

Those who are able to translate and render the future, will be in high demand. The number of data points collected every single day is humongous and it grows exponentially. 'Big data' will be replaced by 'smart data.' And data will no longer just be collected, it will be used actively to make better decisions, develop new projects and ask better questions. It is in this intersection that the need for people, who have learned to think and work with the future and the mindset of a futurist, emerges.

Spotting trends is not the same for everyone. Therefore, it's important that you know what type of futurist you're learning toward. In the process, you must be aware of the connection between the arts and science.

Some people have a well-defined need to document and prove their claims and the movements they've spotted. They lean toward science.

Others are more intuitive and spend their time imagining the future. They lean toward the arts. If you only focus on the arts, your trends will be very dreamy and fluffy like science-fiction, difficult to argue for. Likewise, if you only focus on science, your trends will become a thing of the present with less at risk and, let's be honest, a little boring.

Are You Getting a Divorce? You Financial Advisor Already Knows

The banks are tracking so much data on their customers that they can actually predict if customers are in danger of getting a divorce. This is the qualitative part.

What should the bank do with this knowledge?

This is where the qualitative part comes in. The futurists are those, who can translate this data and put it to good use in inspiring new ways of thinking combinations of trends and the development of scenarios and perspectives.

It might be that the bank expands their services and starts offering getaways for couples, date nights at the cinema or surprises for two. They might also use this insight as an integral part of their family surveillance plan: "We take care of your family's safety and cohesion."

The element of danger inherent in trend spotting is to avoid that your results are used purely on arts or purely on science. Both are necessary in the optimum mix of trends.

In order to avoid ending up in either corners of the ring, you need to embrace your inner futurist type. For example you can be 70/30 science-art. It means that you must be able to present your observations as a part of your argumentation and are ready to jump straight into the future as your present your trends.

Let In Your Inner Futurist

In order to find your unique combination, you must do a small exercise. Some will see it as a wacky gimmick. They are usually the ones, who assess the past and mistake their professional position for their identity. They are often very sceptic and in the worst case, they have a closed mindset. Other people will feel how the exercise forms a foundation for a new perspective on themselves. One that will guide them to create an identity with an enormous drive. This type of person is a lifelong learner, an enquiring soul constantly seeking to develop further. Identity for this type of futurist is something that can be build and knocked down again.

The more you practice designing yourself as a character, the more likely you are to find your core. The core is the ground you stand on, the viewpoint you defend and the things that drive you, the cause for which you'll burn at the stake.

In the movie, 'The Kingdom of Heaven,' the protagonist, Balian, knights a large amount of the men in Jerusalem in order to defend the city.

He tells them, "Be without fear in the face of your enemies. Be brave and upright, that God may love thee. Speak the truth always, even if it leads to your death. Safeguard the helpless and do no wrong; that is your oath. Rise a knight!"

A priest then asks if a man is a better warrior if he has been knighted? To which Balian promptly answers, "Yes!"

The new identity ignites a spark and lights a fire in everyone who used to be carpenters, stable boys and beggars. They're now changed and have been given a new narrative of the future to identify with. In this way, you can have a lot of labels put on you from the outside, but it's your job to make sure they match the magic of your core identity.

Design Your Own Type

The technique we're using to design our own type of futurist is simple. First, choose the skills and characteristics you have right now. Then, you must select two archetype futurists that speak to you and the needs you have in the future. Then, you multiply the parts and get the result. The easiest way is to just write 'Futurist' after your combination. But the cooler version is to create your own unique title.

If you're a qualified auditor, your title might be:

Auditor (expert reviser of financial reports) + former entrepreneur (start-up experience) + voluntary sports coach + prophet (focus on factual predictions) = Revisionary entrepreneur coach, who knows how to check numbers and facts, but who uses them to give advice and predict what is important to his or her key customers, the small and middle-sized entrepreneurs.

If you're a qualified librarian, your title might be:

Librarian + philosopher + oracle = Reinventor of the conversation salons.

It could also be that you're an outdoors expert (with families) + director (multiple-level management) + national team player (activate the body and the team) + explorer (use the future to get to know my self).

Your title would then be Family Ranger, a specialist designer of new ways of being together as a family in the splendid outdoors.

Level 7
VISUALIZATION AND CREATION

BE WHO YOU ARE, UPGRADE YOUR SKILLS AND BECOME RICHER AND FREER

Chapter 10
VISUALIZATION AND CREATION

The distance between what you can imagine and visualize and what can actually be done has never been shorter.

It took coffee about 1,000 years to spread to the whole world. It went from being a religious, muslim drink to being blessed by the Pope. In the 17th century, coffee joined the competition with tea and fought numerous battles to take its current position. Today, if you want a cup of coffee, you can think the thought and produce a cup within minutes.

In 2009, four Spanish students gave themselves a task. They wanted to take pictures of the Earth seen from space. They bought a weather balloon and hooked it to a homemade box that had a camera attached to it, batteries and a tracking sensor. They made sure there wouldn't be any aircrafts in the airspace above them, and so full of helium, the balloon rose up into the air. The gas went off in an altitude of approximately 18 miles and by using Google Earth, the students were able to locate the spot where it came down and landed.

The pictures from the experiment were spectacular. Especially when you consider the price of the experiment, which amounted to a total of about $200. Imagine if NASA were to repeat the experiment. The price would most definitely be higher. Obviously, the quality of the images would be higher, too. But what was the task again? Producing quality shots or shooting pictures of the Earth as seen from space?

The world has changed dramatically since coffee gained world supremacy.

One of the trends that characterizes our time right now is that the distance between imagining things and actually making them happen has never been shorter. That is the platform you're standing on as a futurist. Expect that you've got all the things you need. Expect magic.

The Spanish students used visualization and creative powers to solve the task rather quickly, rather cheap and in a satisfactory quality. And by doing so, they became an amazing example of the fact that the distance between vision and reality really is shorter than ever before. The technology you need is already available and accessible, the skills you need can be learned as you go along, and the demands to financing are usually rather low. Plus, the whole world will applaud you, when you succeed. Magic! To those, who experiment and have their training mindset in place, the world and all the trends and opportunities represent a fun playground.

Unless, of course, you're broke in Bangladesh, but let's get them onboard our rollercoaster ride as well.

The experiment of taking photographs of the Earth from high above has since been copied, for great ideas spread like a wildfire all over the world. A graphic designer sent her son's Thomas the Tank Engine toy into space with a GoPro camera and an animated Thomas face. A pretty epic home video came out of that stunt.

All you need in order to create the future is here, right now. All you need to do is tapping into the energy by combining:

- your vision – your ability to visualize and 'imagining that…" with
- your creative powers – getting your finger out and approaching the work with a trial and error-mindset.

Now, you try. What can you 'imagine …?' The next time you feel your vision and future sense bubbling and buzzing, then take the future for a walk. Be inspired by the above examples and calculate the costs of your first experiment.

And then, go do – while you fight off the demons one after the other.

By using visualization and your creative powers, you can improve the game for the better. You need to be able to win without someone loses. So you must stop spending time on observing your competitors or letting your ego run the show. Instead, show your desire and willingness to change the game itself.

As a futurist, you're training to become a visionary. From now on, when you read about business gurus, talented leaders, successful entrepreneurs and people with big hearts all changing the course of the history, you will know that you, too, may be one of them, if you fuel the tourist and act on the things you see. More rebel, less caretaker.

Don't settle for reports and analyses that are discussed in a studio full of old, sceptic tribal players, who only have yet another depressing conclusion to make, and who encourage 'someone else' to do something about it.

You know that the opportunities to act and do something about it have never been better. And that is why you've already started yourself.

Be the game changer your future needs. How radical would you like it to be?

Who Will Ride Your Wild Horses?

Your MBS is like three horses hitched up to the coach of your life. At the front seat, your ego is running the show. The ego is a real cowboy, typical of Tribal. The ego is easily seduced by material goods, status, and acknowledgement. If everyone else gets a golden coach, he wants one, too. If the latest fashion trend is a new cowboy hat, he will insist that we pull over and go shopping before we can move on. The ego can create so many interruptions, if you don't stop to say, "Hey pal, thank you very much for taking care of everybody. But remember your job is to steer the horses in the direction of our magical vision."

Your ego doesn't have to be your enemy, though. Instead, you can dress him/her up to be your loyal servant reminding you to enjoy life, receive what you have earned and make room for the acknowledgement you get. You body is here to live life to the fullest, so do welcome all the good that comes your way. And enjoy! (And watch out for the Procrastinator, too).

You've completed level 7, when you know how to control your ego.

New Skills

If you want to upgrade your skills and be richer and freer, you will need to upgrade your futurist by installing a training mindset.

In this book, we share the trick of how to become a full-blown futurist. What's interesting is that you already have what you need to be one. But if you don't know how to put it all to good use, nothing will ever will happen. If you are in a car and you don't know that there's something called keys, you'll just sit at the front seat mimicking the sound of the engine, "WROOOOOOUUUUM!" You will not ask for things you don't know exist. Others will look at you and think you lack the motivation, the self-confidence or is coming down with stress.

In reality, you just need the keys and learn how to start the car. It won't take five minutes, but once you've learned, it'll make a big difference.

The next step is the actual driving. Others can teach you the theory and the basic techniques, but you'll never be able to pick it up in this way alone. Only practice and training. It takes days and months to become a good driver.

Provide two sloppy chefs with the best ingredients in the world and they'll still fuck it up. Give two great chefs $50, on the other hand, drop them off by the edge of the woods and come back later to enjoy a feast.

The best investment is to identify the most wanted skills in the future related to the person you want to be and then start practicing today. Being good at something and being able to unlearn and learn again is the best insurance you can have. Nothing provides peace of mind as knowing that you can master a skill the world needs, and which makes you truly happy. That and being in a community of people who see and like you, just as you are.

Competence is good for you. And for others. Competent people want to hang out with competent people in buddy teams and dedicated communities. If you're a boss, you need talented employees. Elite athletes, musicians and artists practice and rehearse their ass off in order to become the most talented in the world. We want our children to do well in school and cultivate hobbies to be able to excel at something that might only be meaningful to ourselves.

Mastering a craft will bring into play the cards on your hand. Whether or not you're God's gift to mankind or the smartest tool in the box, it doesn't matter. You're not meant to hold your cards tight, you're supposed to put yourself into action. Acquire new skills throughout your life, so you'll be able to play the best possible hand. At any time.

Human beings have reinvented themselves since the beginning of time. And now we have to do it more often and faster. So, let's make it as fun and rewarding as possible! More computer gaming, less Monopoly.

Instead of a skills upgrade or taking another 6 months course, we must be better at resolving the most important problems and the most crucial tasks ahead of us, and do it quick. We need to be able to crack the code and acquire new skills, no matter where we are in life. School is never out and its no longer just a physical room or building. School is a mental space.

So, what does it mean, cracking the code? In order to explain this, we'll use the principle of the lever, a great technique, which for thousands of years made it possible for people to accomplish tasks that were so much bigger than what they and their bodies were able to manage.

For a futurist, competence consists of three things: technique, method and perseverance.

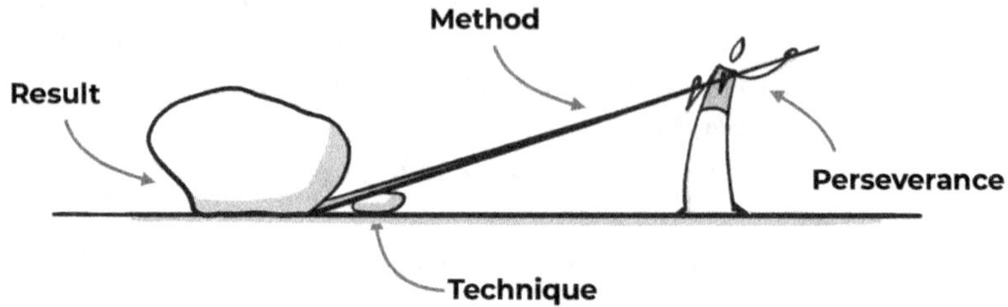

Technique is the right way of doing things. Usually, it will only take a few minutes to communicate. If the door to the gate of wisdom is locked, the technique is the key you need to be able to unlock it and enter the room of learning.

The method is what you choose to do once you step into the room of learning. The method is your personal and unique take on the technique, and it will take minutes or days to adopt a new technique into your catalogue of learning.

Perseverance is the ability to never give up on a bad day. Without perseverance, only a very few things would stick in your procedural memory.

Riding a bicycle is easy to explain as a technique: Get up, grab the steer, pedal and keep your balance. And break when you need to.

But nobody learns how to ride a bicycle just by being told the simple how-tos of it. You have to get up and pedal, make your own mistakes and ride the bike in a way that's meaningful to you. You need to find your own personal method.

So, perseverance is the factor that determines if you can drop the stabilizing training wheels, and later in life, it becomes the difference between a hobby bicyclist and a professional racing cyclist.

Talent in this case is just a head start. A gift that somebody did or did not unwrap. Very few people are allowed to shine with their talent.

Others go through the first 20 years of their life applauding from the road side only to burn out, because they didn't learn how to handle a conflict, setbacks or injustice – because they didn't train their perseverance.

It's easy to take the example of the 1% of humanity, for whom everything seems to succeed. The truth is that to 99% of the world's population, success is gained through persisting and hard work. And because perseverance is so important, it's even more important that you get it right from the beginning.

Cracking the code is to be good at adapting new techniques. The technique is the little rock, the small difference that keeps you from wasting hours and hours of hard work and training without getting the result you deserve. When you begin with the technique, you make sure to rehearse and practice the right things. The technique should also give some sort of redemption or magic moment. The feeling of creation that makes you think like Pippi Longstocking; "I've never tried this before, so I think I should definitely be able to do that."

For, what is the difference between Tina and Ken from your school? Tina is the well-prepared girl, who always studies very hard and feels like she does everything right, but never really gets the grades nor the acknowledgement, she deserves. And then there's Ken, who aces all of his papers without doing a day's work and who gets one great grade after another in spite of his partying, skiing holidays and an after-school job.

So, is Tina dumber than Ken? Is Ken more talented (and charming) than Tina?

The answer is that Ken learned from a very early age that you have to get the technique right in order to avoid working your fingers to the bone to get the result you want. Tina, on the other hand, thinks that she needs to work hard and diligently, before she can harvest the fruit (without feeling guilty) and that the hard work in itself is a guarantee of success.

Worst case for Ken is that he won't develop resilience. His weakness will be perseverance, because he has become used to things coming easily to him. Whenever he experiences setbacks, because the tasks of life are getting heavier and heavier or more complicated, his spine is simply too weak. Then Ken will begin to think that something's wrong with him, unless his buddy comes to his rescue.

Worst case for Tina is to end up like a well-meaning and educated academic. She'll make thrifty, laborious, wise and dedicated contributions to reports, analyses and dissertations together with other thrifty, laborious and well-meaning people. Her method lever will be longer and longer, but it will never leave the ground. She won't help solve any important problems or serve the community, and if the right technique or task should land on her table, her lever has now become so long that she has lost her grounding.

You must tell you inner Tina that hard work never falls out of fashion, but that it is dangerous to wear blinkers and work hard without checking first if there might be a better way to do things. Also ask, if the one thing that Tina is really good at isn't something that a robot might do instead?

You should also remind you inner Ken that there's a certain beauty and releasing factor about making a pledge and committing to a cause, for he needs to be careful not to trip over the many amazing opportunities the future has to offer. Don't surf superficially in and out of online master classes or do a seminar here and there. And don't enrol for a degree that doesn't let you absorb the material and contemplate.

It's all about balancing the competence account:

- What problem(s) are you solving?
- Are you using the right technique?
- How much time did you set aside?
- Are you motivated to work on it?
- Are you interested in learning how to master a new method?
- How will you feel when you've become quite good at this?
- How has your life improved?
- What are you willing to sacrifice?
- How persevering are you?
- Do you need a buddy or a framework that makes you stick to your cause, when things get really hard?

You have your whole life to ponder the question of 'what you should like to be good at.' And if in doubt, just focus on becoming better. At something. For, if you have learned to master one skill, it's far more easy to master everything else. And this is contagious, for talented people never fall out of fashion either.

And talented people wants to be with other talented people. Making a community pledge.

Three Ways to Get Stuck in a Level

In this book, we've given you the techniques and the principles to move up a level as a planetary futurist and game changer. But you need to translate these techniques into your own life and develop your own method. You must take responsibility for your perseverance, the practice, for it is this principle that will determine how good you'll be. And then you need to act on the things you see and make the changes necessary. In order to make it easier for you, we've identified three ways to get stuck in a level out of a lack of tangible tools. Hopefully, this will help you to get your game moving.

The toiler: lousy technique, strong method and perseverance. Long lever, no small rock.

If you have a long lever (method), but lack the fundamental technique, you risk spending a big part of your life trying to get the wrong things right. You've got perseverance and you do educate further. Unfortunately, you are not able to feel in your gut what to do with all that accumulated knowledge.

Your culprit is Complex Rex: big head, way to short arms. In the end, your lever will be so long that it will knock you in your huge head. Or else you'll cling to your method in such a way that you lose your grounding. Which is in fact double trouble. Spending so much energy on doing so little and then experiencing that it's your own method and perseverance that hold you back? Dude!

The way to move forward is to put down you lever and start challenging yourself on the techniques. Find the little things that makes the task so much easier. Being smart is not cheating! And, if it feels easy, you're most likely back on track.

The idler: great technique, average method, and no perseverance.

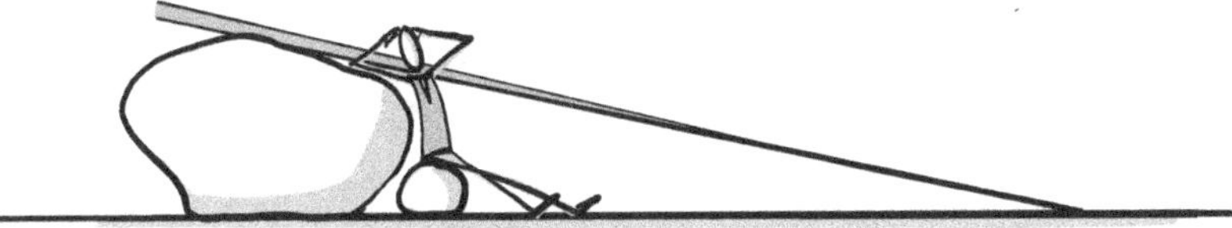

Here's a person, who cracked the code, but unfortunately didn't learn to try hard, which is why she perceives setbacks as a sign that she's in a wrong place.

Her job, relationship or the challenge she was so enthusiastic about two minutes ago has suddenly become too hard and/or boring. A sign from above that she needs to re-saddle and she's again cheerfully posting about her change of scenery on social media.

As a young person, people saw great potential in her, but in time it's faded away. Instead, it has become normal for her to start new projects, where she can shine her light, and then jump on to the next, before routines, or the long haul, again enters her life.

The idler may develop into a smart ass, who knows all the fundamental principles, technique and theories, but who never dug deeper herself and became really good at something. This is why she so easily underestimates how much time a task requires, and why she more often than not acts condescending toward the effort of others.

The idler will release her potential, when she hooks up with a buddy, who can remind her of absorption and obligation, when she becomes part of a community who loves to see her stink and fight her way through boredom, and where failing and being truly challenged is more cool than being too smart too quick. Maybe she already joined a bicycle club or a gym, where she will feel the joy in making an effort or bear pain. Just because it's hard, it doesn't mean it's wrong.

The weightlifter: small rock, lots of perseverance, and way too big a task.

The weightlifter is a perfectionist, who's unconsciously good a cracking the code, fairly good on method and who gets his primary workgasm from doing heavy lifting for a long period of time.
The weightlifter takes it all upon himself and works his ass off. He's happy to get up before he even went to bed and he works well on his own. The problem is that the world around him tends to add bigger and bigger task to his load, and the weightlifter doesn't know how to say, 'No!' And then he comes down with stress. And begins to feel guilty. When that happens, he begins to work on his stress like it's another burden to bear. Run it out.

The weightlifter will feel a big redemption when he takes a tiny break and recognizes that big tasks must be solved in groups and that being able to collaborate with others, leading others and creating an amazing team is just as formidable as solving a problem by yourself. For the weightlifter, the code will be cracked when he learns how to relax and accept the world for what it is. And when he realizes that other people can solve the problem just as fine, perhaps even better, in their own way.

It's not a weakness to ask for help or delegate tasks!

The Stinking Stage & Mini Goals

When you find yourself going through hell, keep going. And stick with the contract you make with yourself. You can't be good at anything without stinking at first. As you begin to play the Game of the Future (well anything new, really), you'll reach the stinking stage sooner or later. It usually happens when you're overwhelmed by the many tasks of life and when your trend observations frustrate you, when complexity overhauls your level of intelligence, your co-workers are fired, the boss changes the course of action, the kids are impossible and it feels like the world is against you… and your head is about to explode.

Then you stink!

The stinking stage arrives, when your brain has understood something your body has not yet internalized and it doesn't know how to convert this new knowledge into action. It's a phase you live through, just like Winston Churchill said, "If you're going through hell, keep going!"

In the stinking stage, the sheep are separated from the goats, because this is the point where most people give up. Everybody can join in the first phase with excitement, that's easy. But when the going gets tough, boring, hard or difficult, the majority opts out. When the first infatuation with the future has evaporated, the diffuse complexity of the many trends and the new set of tasks become too overwhelming. Before you throw in the towel, however, know that before a breakthrough there is a breakdown.

If you're not ready to let go, you can't seize the new. At this point, it's about getting your shit together and pull through. Or, letting go and let fall what cannot stand.

The good news is that when you stink, you're actually better than when you felt good. Huh? Yes, hear us out. Say we return to the metaphor of riding a bicycle. At this point, you're mastering the level of the training wheel. Yay, excitement all over and then, boring right?

Then you advanced to the next level without training wheels. And then you stink again, but you've actually become better at riding a bike, even though it doesn't feel that way!

Stink 100%

The world is full of trends that are threatening and dangerous. And in these years, the crises are queueing up: refugees, environment, nature, health, terrorism, etc. Is it even possible to save the planet? Good people feel a natural responsibility to act, but our actions seem petty and banal.

When complexity overhauls the intelligence, you can do one of two things.

GIVE IT UP, GOD DAMN IT!

GIVE IT UP!
LET GO, GO HOME AND BINGE-WATCH
A SEASON OF MASTERCHEF INSTEAD.

Or, you can say:

"WELL, WELL."

"AHA."

"INTERESTING."

Soon, you'll experience the value of staying in the game. Even though you don't have the faintest clue about what's going on, or you don't know what to do. If you did, you'd probably already have done it, right?

Baby steps are also steps, so commit to doing small, but productive
things. Toward something better. To you and yours. Something you
can do every day for 60 seconds or 15 minutes. And when you've done
it, you're done – for today.

It might be that you're spending 5 minutes of your commute observing
and taking notes. During the meeting, you can wonder why people
do what they do. You can also take pictures of your magic moments
or ask a great question, before you go to bed and fall asleep. Or, you
can read a book about something you want to learn and which has
nothing to do with the things you've trained for all your life. Maybe,
a bicyclist spits on your car and you feel the urge to throw your tribal
ax. But instead you spend five minutes exploring where that came
from. People who do things like that don't have a surplus of energy.
They had a bad day and might be stuck in a series of automated chain
reactions, which you can reverse by yelling, "You are soooo beautiful
and hooooooooot!" after them.

By committing to these little things, you remain in the Game of the
Future. As Gandalf says in 'The Lord of the Rings' in an answer
to the question of why he picked a mere hobbit as the chosen one:
"Saruman believes it is only great power that can hold evil in check,
but that is not what I have found. It is the small everyday deeds of
ordinary folk that keep the darkness at bay. Small acts of kindness and
love. Why Bilbo Baggins? Perhaps because I am afraid, and he gives
me courage."

Small acts of kindness and love. Maybe it's all it takes for us to go
from Tribal to Planetary? And someone has to go first. It takes roughly
about 100 days for your brain to adjust to a new habit. So with a small
effort a couple of minutes every day, you'll have a new and magical
brain, wired to open the many opportunities of the future to you and
help you see and feel what will be important, and to believe that you
are good and important enough to act on the things you see.

Does that sound like a good investment?
We think so!

And we encourage you to write down your mini goals down. For, when you put things down in writing, it's easier to keep up your good intentions. The things you need to do every day and which will take only about a minute:

My mini goal(s):

____

____

CHAPTER 11

CONGRATULATIONS!

YOU'VE WON THE GAME OF THE FUTURE

To infinity and beyond… as Buzz Lightyear says.

The Star Wars movie, 'A New Hope,' ends with a big ceremony with fanfares and the whole shebang. The heroes, Luke Skywalker and Han Solo, are honored with medals for their contribution to destroying the first Death Star of the Empire.

In the same way, we honor you. You are well on you way to destroy the Death Star of tribalism and lead humanity toward a new and better planetary future.

Chapter 11
Congratulations!
YOU'VE WON THE GAME OF THE FUTURE

If we were to boil down this book to the utmost essentials, we'd like to pass on seven points that we hope you'll take with you.

1. You are now able to see the future (before everyone else). Trends are everywhere. You'll read about them in the news. They're discussed in the media by journalists and politicians, they make up the difference between success and failure for a company, and they are the very essence when big decisions are on the table. Trends have always shaped the world, and now they do it quicker than ever before. People like you, who know how to see, catch and argue for the future, will be in very high demand!

2. You've awaken and developed your future sense. Working with trends is equal parts art and equal parts science. Art is where you personality enters the picture. It's where you sense the future in your own unique way. Intuition and gut feeling can't be copied, and if you do well, you'll be outsmarting the robots. The future is like an endless sea, and if you believe you have to understand it before you can make a decision, it will be like drinking the entire ocean before you go for a swim. Let go of your need to understand everything. Historically, most of the big inventions and breakthroughs we know happened by mistake. Without misunderstandings, no progress. You'll make the world a huge favor, when you dare to travel into the unknown with your future sense head first. When you're being curious and believe in the things we can't yet see.

3. You've created you own way of being a futurist. Since the beginning of time, seven different archetypes have helped people gaining a sense of the future. You can channel the strengths from all of them. There's no one-size fits all when it comes to spotting trends. You must design your own style, your own magic in how you observe, how you collect data, how you design trends and how you argue for and about the future with others. Actually, you can say that you are the destination for the journey into the future!

4. Your boss loves you. Just like your kids, your partner and your friends. Because you have become a better, more open and less annoyed listener. As a futurist, you don't care who's right and who's wrong. You are far more preoccupied with what's interesting and what arguments you need to make in order to get others to win the future with you. Different segments need different arguments. Some wants to be seduced, others want professionalism. Everyone needs to hear news about the future in a way that doesn't scare the shit out of them, but gives them hope and the freedom to act. As you begin to master the skill, you become the most inspiring person at any gathering.

5. You make better decisions and you don't have to make 300 of them every day. Maybe just settle for one or two, three really great ones. You can find the trends that will shape your life and be so much ahead of them that you can design the future you want, including letting go of the past, of taboos and the big box of mental Christmas ornaments you really don't need anymore.

6. You're not the only weirdo anymore. People, who can see the future, often feel like aliens. The visionary, the intuitive, the psychic have all been ridiculed, persecuted and even killed for being who they are and their urge to asking questions and changing the status quo. But never again. For the world will be increasingly connected. You're no longer a crazy nutter. You are now part of a global community of futuristic friends, who love and appreciate you just as you are.

7. And you can help change the rules of the game, from Tribal to
   Planetary. When you use your future sense to act on the future
   you see, because you've been called to it and you know that this is
   where your magic is, then you change the world, then you become
   the game changer. Step proudly into the long row of little big
   heroes, who changed the game for the better for us all – before,
   now and in the future.

The Universe of the Future
– The Big Overview

Words and concepts that will help planetary futurists communicate
with each other.

A TREND

A development, movement or observation, which like a big or small
transformation has the power and capacity to change the way we
think, feel, work, act, priorities or experience the world.

Trends may be small waves: quickly over, yet with a potential to
swallow a lot of attention, like for instance in fashion, a funny app or
the latest dooms day scenario.

Trends may also be long-lasting waves that influence and change
the way a whole group of people view the world: A theory of
management or society's attitudes towards children's education,
gender roles and sexuality. Trends can also be undercurrents, powerful
and everlasting, like sustainability and automatization.

You can also think of trends like pieces in a puzzle. One piece, one
trend in itself, rarely makes sense. But the more you gather, collect
and identify and the more time you spend letting your future brain
putting the pieces together, the easier it will be for you to see the bigger
picture.

HARD TREND

A trend which is very likely to have an impact on your life. Hard trends are the terms and conditions of the future. And you shouldn't take it personally. It just happens. A hard trend is the wave that is headed directly toward you, whether you like it or not.

Rule of thumb: If you ask if you have a choice, the answer is "No!" with hard trends. You can't decide if a trend is hard or soft without a time frame and a vantage point.

SOFT TREND

A trend, which is interesting, frustrating, funny, hyped, annoying or in some other way sets the cat among the pigeons.

Rule of thumb: If you ask if you have a choice, the answer is "Yes!" You need to act on the soft trends in order for them to happen.

Soft trends are not necessarily going to have an impact on you, but they represent the many opportunities in life and the diversity of the world. Welcome them, especially the trends that keep popping up in your head. Take a closer look at them. A soft trend is the wave you expect and which you decide to ride along.

MEGA TREND

An impressive trend, which is often made up of other trends. A few drops become a pool that becomes the wave of the mega trend. Mega trends can be soft or hard, but they are characterized by showing up when the big boys in class agree that we're dealing with a mega trend. Because mega trends are promoted in the media, they often become self-fulfilling prophecies. The fourth industrial revolution is an example of a new dominating mega trend.

Urbanization, the fact that people all over the world are seeking a life in the big cities, have been a mega trend for a long period of time. The leaders of the world, construction firms and politicians treat urbanization like a hard trend, like a condition, but actually it's not. There are a lot of countertrends. Urbanization can be turned if enough people believe that happiness can be found outside the city life.

Mega trends are comparable with ocean currents. They are the biggest movements, but they are found beneath the waves and push everything on the surface. This is the reason why it's often more interesting to look at the waves (trends), which the mega trend helps developping.

COUNTERTRENDS OR ANTI-TRENDS

An opposing response to another trend. A response to being online on social media all the time is, for instance, the trend of 'digital detox' – going offline for a weekend, for a week, or maybe just one night. The countertrend is important to consider, because it often shows where the resources are scarce.

When we see a wave peaking in the media and the 24/7 news stream, the countertrend will show a need for the opposite. In this case, it can be tailor-made attention and thoughtfulness in for instance book clubs for books that are out of print. The countertrend is the wave that hits back after it has peaked. Out in the ocean, all waves appear to be moving up and down, but by the shore, they move back and forth. It's on the top of the wave that the new drive emerges. Not as a static movement, but as a dynamic movement.

GAME CHANGER

The trend with the biggest potential to disrupt or transform you or you industry. When you find you game changer, the future sits really close. It will feel like it zooms in on you. The game changer in journalism is algorithms and robots that write better texts, do more thorough research and check facts, while the game changer for cab drivers is self-driving cars. The game changer can wipe out an entire industry, if you don't upgrade the human skill set. But it also represents a huge potential for innovation and reinventions.

A game changer in the visual universe can be observed when the water withdraws and we try to get it back. Compare it to the tsunami on the beach. Before it hits with a second wave, it clears away all the water.

If you respond to a game changer and change the course of history, you are the game changer.

These are the most important concepts in the universe of the futurist. If you want a better sense of the future, you should also know the following.

CYCLIC TRENDS

Trends that look like something we've seen before. Trends do not repeat, but they can rhyme. Like for instance the green movement and the sharing economy that remind us of the hippies in the 1970s, or populism and demagogs in politics, who resemble the period leading up to the Second World War.

Cyclic trends are portrayed in the classic way of drawing up waves. They go up and down, up and down. This frequency is the cycle of the waves.

EXPONENTIAL TRENDS

Trends that move slowly at first and then clear out fast, which is the reason why we tend to overestimate or even reject them in the short run and underestimate them in the long run. Social media spread at the speed of light, even though only few people were able to imagine what the Internet, text messages or iPads could be used for. Computer games like PokemonGo and Fortnite followed the same curve. Artificial Intelligence, 3D-printing, intelligent fridges and unschooling all have the potential to do the same.

Exponential trends are the waves that surfers ride on. They only show their fun potential, when we, who choose to ride along, step on it to go full speed ahead. And then it's too late for the inflatable beach toy at the beach.

WILD CARD

Trends that are less likely to materialize, but which, if they do, change the world radically. We might also refer to them as unrealistic game changers. A wild card would be if science manages to somehow prove the existence of God or finds out how to annihilate gravity. Or if aliens come to visit. Or if democratic processes were hijacked by dodgy data consultants.

Wildcards can push your audience to the edge of their imagination. They can do so, because wildcards provoke the futuristic brain up in gear, where we allow ourselves to work with the unexpected, the unrealistic and the truly unique things that may or may never happen.

A wildcard is the meteor that hits the water, explodes and changes everything.

THE RULES OF THE GAME

The rules of the game are our fundamental presumptions about how the world works. Trends challenge the status quo and hard trends always challenge the existing power structures. We all live in the same reality, but some of us are better at reading trends than others, because they understand the rules of the game and can move faster and easier toward their goals. A rule of thumb is that if life is experienced as tough, unfair and it seems like everyone else is cheating, it's time to update your basic assumptions about how things work, your ground rules. The rules of the game is that part of the ocean where we build our raft, set up a home with a satellite dish. Where we agree on a code of conduct and who is in charge.

VISION

A visualization of your future, often your most desired version. Being a visionary is to be able to imagine that things can look very different. A vision is constantly moving. And a good vision motivates you to work with the things you don't yet know exist, and it must be able to stop you from automatically steering toward solutions and thoughts you already know. Your vision is the story that lifts us above the ocean, so we may see the world from a bird's-eye perspective. It's what you see, feel and believe. It's what encourages us to embark on new adventures.

TENDENCY

Tendencies are events that may result in a trend. In this way, it takes several examples of the same event to make one trend. Tendencies are drops of water in the ocean, the new water that the waves are made of.

PROGNOSIS

The projection of existing trends, statistics or movements. Prognoses often begin with the sentence: "If this development continues, then…" and the curve is prolonged.

We know prognoses from the weather, elections and population growth. They often make sense in terms of technology. Unfortunately, the prognosis is also often abused in the media. For example, a rubric like, "The number of surrogate mothers is increasing," might be true if the number one year goes up from 8 to 64. But that doesn't mean that the number next year will be 4,096 and in two years 16,777, 216.

The prognosis describes whether or not a wave in the short run continues in a certain direction and its potential consequences.

FORECASTING

In a forecasting, trends are projected without too much creativity, which is why forecasts often end up as caricatures of reality, in utopias and dystopias. If you use a few good trend cards in your forecasting, you'll find new connections in relation to your existing challenges. You can explore the consequences of the decision you already made, assess your blind spots and figure out where to invest in the future.

A forecasting describes how the wave will move and the consequences it might have in the long run.

BACKCASTING

We like to exercise hindsight and we'll often say things like, "I knew it!" This statement is a proof that your futuristic brain was at work. You just lacked the skill to communicate in a way that made your audience pay attention, or it might be that you weren't very clear about your sense of the future. In backcasting, we dissect historical events to find hard and soft trends as well as the game changer. By learning from history and practicing the ability to spot who saw the consequences first, what happened to them, what was destroyed and created, we can train our futuristic muscles to recognizing the same factors in the present and in the future.

Backcasting is the story about the ocean and the waves that used to be and the learning and experiences we can gain from those experiences.

DISRUPTION

Disruption is when the future arrives earlier than anticipated and very quickly moves to disturb or destroy your business model. The term is very often misunderstood and so it calls on our worst fears. Many people talking about disruption use the term like a hand grenade tossed into the room, which will make most decision-makers shut down and go in survival mode. Disruption in a more edible version can showcase several possible futures and the opportunity to do something about it.

Emotional Encyclopedia for Planetary Futurists

Use Your Feelings as Navigators

In Tribal, it's normal that you let your thoughts and feelings control you. This makes it difficult to deal with dilemmas as emotions are personal, brief and diffuse. The things you want to do, like staying in bed late, binge-watching TV-shows and having snacks for breakfast, are not always what makes you truly happy. And the things that make you happy, like exercising, calling your parents, opening pane envelopes, are not always what you feel most like doing.

One of the reasons why a lot of people don't use their emotions right is that we're not used to talking about them. We take it way too personally and think that we are wrong for being 'this emotional,' too much or too little, or that our emotions don't deserve the attention. We push them aside or try to protect each other's emotions.

Players in the Tribal mode like to collect things of emotional importance. Some evolves into hoarders, who'll never let go of the past, as in 'not in a million years.' They let their emotions define them so that, for instance, they are 'a person suffering from anxiety,' which really is an inclination to being kiddy offended over the littlest things. On that note, why is it called 'menstruation' and not 'womenstruation'? That's just not good enough!

When we hide away our emotions and thoughts and keep them in the dark, our feelings develop feelings of their own. This results in you feeling guilty for being sad or that you hate yourself for feeling desire. Budding emotions are a load of horse shit! But shit is merely energy at a disgusting stage. With a planetary twist, our emotions can become the most fierce fertilizer boosting our creative powers.

In Planetary, your emotions are an integral part of your MBS. You just have to allow yourself to feel your feelings. Greet them with a hug and a warm "well, well." You'll never be able to control them anyway, but they'll be able to guide you if you are able to decode the message. Cough up your feelings like a cat coughs up hair balls. Hold them out and examine them and try to figure out what they're trying to tell you. How can this poop of emotion fertilize and boost your dreams? What do you need to do to heal the wounds of your inner child or the things that he or she is looking for in everything else?

Know that you are not your thoughts and emotions. The future you're about to enter will change who you are. So, come on, leave all the unnecessary thoughts and emotions behind and go chase that game changer you so desperately want to be.

En route toward that person, you should pay special attention to your feelings. Sometimes, feelings are just fart, but sometimes they're also a gold nugget full of enlightenment and meaning that provide new perspectives and a great view. If only you'll listen louder.

ANGER
Think: My values and principles are being challenged. Where do I hold my ground and what am I fighting for?

ANXIETY
Think: Anxiety is anger I don't express because I don't know who I am. I need to define my principles and values, my vantage point, and be more extroverted. And by the way, I can't be brave if I'm not also a little scared.

APATHETIC
Think: My creative powers have come to a halt and I can't get anything started. I think. Actually, I don't know. Where in my life do I have something cooking?

Where do I feel the magic? And how can I convince myself that I have as much right to be here as everybody else?

BAD CONSCIENCE

Think: I'm doing the best I can. And I am allowed, actually it's my duty, to spend time creating my own zone of safety, my own island and vision, my own energy. When I do that, I generate so much surplus energy that I can share it with others.

BITCHING

Think: I need to get rid of this feeling. I have to find someone I can carp and nag with. Yum, yum, it's going to be fun to just spill whatever pisses me off. But then I'll be done bitching!

CONFUSED

Think: Welcome to the real world! There will be more and more entropy (a fancy word for chaos) in the universe, and I won't be able to control any of it… and I don't have to. I need to let go and lean into the knowledge, guidance and action – the things that are happening in my time.

CRITICAL

Think: The best possible way to be sceptic, which is far more proactive than being worried. If I can't be neutral, it's okay to be critical, curious and ask questions.

CURIOSITY

Think: Look at how good I am. Curiosity is the most important feeling a futurist may have. What do I want to explore, investigate, examine and discover, just because I can?

DISAPPOINTMENT

Think: I'll just spend some time getting it out of my system, saying, "Never mind" and take full responsibility. The person, who takes the blame, gets the right to act. Tomorrow, I'll spend my time and energy on magic and not on the things that went wrong yesterday.

EMBITTERED

Think: No headhunter is going to see me any time soon. So I'll go traveling or throw a party, so I can gain new perspectives and stop ploughing the same furrow for a while.

ENVY

Think: I wouldn't long for it, if it wasn't within my reach. This person knows something I have an aptitude for. What doesn't this person represent to me?

EXALTED

Think: Life is an amusement park. And I am so happy, so, so happy. Still, I don't need to try out all the rides. Instead, I'll use my excitement and creative powers on the things I know are good for me.

FRUSTRATION

Think: Hang on, hang on! Before a breakthrough there's always a breakdown. I actually need to go where I'm optimally frustrated. Frustration is very often just passion without a plan or a system. Who can help me make a plan?

GRATEFUL

Think: I'm paying my debt to the universe. When I make an effort to take a break and feel really grateful, and not just skate around it, the universe will understand what I'd like more of.

HATRED

Think: Hatred is like drinking poison and hoping that the others will die. Instead, I forgive. I want to practice finding the good in other people, no matter how big a demon sits on their shoulder.

HOPEFUL

Think: It's important (and difficult) being so full of hope and a little naive. When it comes own to it, courage really is just a lacking sense of reality. Hope comes before courage.

INDIGNATION

Think: I am pissed on behalf of the world. What can or must I do to help others? Whose fight am I fighting?

INSULTED OR OFFENDED

Think: Being insulted or offended is the modern version of being cross. I know there's no justice in the world besides the one I help create. Still, I can never have enough of that I want, so now I go all in on creating what I want to see in the world.

IRRITATION

Think: Okay, there's something here I don't want to know. What is the message I need to pay more attention to? How is that annoying asshole right?

LONELY

Think: I feel lonely, but I am not alone. Everything in the universe is connected and when I understand who I am, I'll hook up with people, who are good for me.

MAGIC MOMENTS

Think: I am where I need to be, and I want more! Mmmmh, I soak in it and reload a little magic into my cells. More of that, please!

SCEPTIC

Think: There is very little energy, hope and trust in being sceptic.
I'll move up a level in energy and will be critical, curious, and asking
questions instead. I'll follow my wonder and look for innovations
instead of letting the bitter confirmation that nothing is possible run
the show.

TIRED

Think: It's perfectly okay. I'm allowed to be tired and my brain needs
me to take a nap, go for a walk or chill on the couch.

TRUST

Think: I'm so lucky! When I have trust, I can rely on the fact that
there's something or someone out there, who wants what's best for me.
Mmmmh, what a luxury, let me have some more.

WORRY

Think: Worry is the lowest feeling in the universe. It's asking for the
things I don't want. I want to practice thinking about all the things
that may go well. And I'll write down my worries and for each one
of them, I'll note the good things that can happen. In this way my
worries become my safety net

FUTURE SENSE

New World – New Game Rules
May the Force of the Future Be With You

Anne Skare Nielsen & Henrik Good Hovgaard
in collaboration with Søren Frandsen

English translation: Hannah Bergqvist,
share@hannahbergqvist.com

© Universal Futurist, 2020

1st edition
ISBN: 978-87-972389-1-2

Layout, graphics and illustrations: Henrik Good Hovgaard

Printed at Scandinavian Books

Copyright rules
Universal Future
Nordstrands Allé 4
2791 Dragør
Danmark]